A Path to Degenerative Development

MABIRA FOREST GIVEAWAY

TONY AKAKI

iUniverse, Inc.
Bloomington

Mabira Forest Giveaway
A Path to Degenerative Development

iUniverse books may be ordered through booksellers or by contacting:

iUniverse
1663 Liberty Drive
Bloomington, IN 47403
www.iuniverse.com
1-800-Authors (1-800-288-4677)

ISBN: 978-1-4620-1728-7 (sc)
ISBN: 978-1-4620-1730-0 (hc)
ISBN: 978-1-4620-1729-4 (e)

Printed in the United States of America

iUniverse rev. date: 2/13/2012

The first mega-crisis in Uganda, however, will
not come from a dispute over stolen votes or oil revenue.
It is likely to be caused by the environment.

Charles Onyango-Obbo

Foreword by Princess Jane Mpologoma

In August 2006, Ugandan President Yoweri Museveni commissioned the National Forestry Authority (NFA) to undertake a feasibility study of clearing 7,100 hectares of the Mabira forest so that the Sugar Corporation of Uganda (SCOUL), which is owned by the Mehta Group, could grow more sugarcane. The president defended this action in an article, "Why I Support Mabira Forest Give-Away to Mehta Group."

Many Ugandans were opposed to and enraged by the government's move to destroy part of one of Uganda's biggest forests. Opposition to the giveaway led to public demonstrations in April 2007, which led to destruction of property and loss of life. The Mabira demonstrations were the most egalitarian in Uganda's history, with people of all classes, ages, and political affiliations taking part.

The NFA report commissioned by the president concluded that the ecological and long-term economic losses from destroying almost a fourth of the forest would be a disaster. It is clear that the destruction of Uganda's forests raises complex socioeconomic, environmental, and cultural questions. Forest destruction in Buganda is a concern to me, and Tony Akaki's book is a welcome contribution to opening up constructive dialogue on economic development and the environment. On this issue, one cannot remain silent, and to quote Dante, "the hottest places in Hell are reserved for those who, in a time of great moral crisis, maintain their neutrality."

Uganda's forestry policy is based on a number of principles that build on the government's national development priorities of poverty eradication and good governance, one of which is the consideration of cultural and traditional attributes and institutions. This has been overlooked, as in Buggala subcounty on the Ssese Islands, where indigenous trees in the Luggo forests are cut down in favor of palm trees to the benefit of oil-producing companies. This has been a concern to me, as the Ddamula,

To

A. Milton Akaki

Table of Contents

Acronyms and Abbreviations

AII Africa Innovations Institute

BUCADEF Buganda Cultural and Development Foundation

CBD Convention on Biological Diversity

CCD Convention to Combat Desertification

CITES Convention on International Trade in Endangered Species of Wild Fauna and Flora

COMESA Common Market of Eastern and Southern Africa

CPI Corruption Perception Index

DRC Democratic Republic of Congo

EIA Environment Impact Assessment

FAO Food and Agricultural Organization

FCPF Forest Carbon Partnership Facility

GDP Gross Domestic Product

GNP Gross National Product

HFCS High-Fructose Corn Syrup

HIPC Heavily Indebted Poor Countries

ICJ International Court of Justice

IDP Internally Displaced Persons

IDRC International Development Research Centre

KSB Kenya Sugar Board

KSREF Kenya Sugar Research Foundation

LRA Lord's Resistance Army

MISP Multi-Stakeholder Integrative Sustainability Planning

NAPE National Association of Professional Environmentalists

NCAR National Center for Atmospheric Research

NEMA National Environment Management Authority

NFA National Forestry Authority

NGO Nongovernmental Organization

NRM National Resistance Movement

ODA Overseas Development Assistance

OECD Organization for Economic Cooperation and Development

REDD Reduced Emissions from Deforestation and Degradation

SARS Severe Acute Respiratory Syndrome

SIPC Severely Indebted Poor Countries

SME Small and Medium Enterprises

UCOTA Uganda Community Tourism Association

UIA Uganda Investment Authority

UNCED United Nations Conference on Environment and Development

UNDP United Nations Development Programme

UNFCCC United Nations Framework Convention on Climate Change

UNICEF United Nations Children's Fund

UPDF Uganda Peoples Defence Forces

USAID United States Agency for International Development

WHO World Health Organization

WWF World Wildlife Fund

Chapter 1

THE FUTURE IS NOT A GIFT

The future is not a gift: it is an achievement.
Every generation helps make its own future.
This is the essential challenge of the present.

Robert F. Kennedy

The future is not a gift that the present generation or government can bequest to the following generations. International legal instruments often refer to the "rights of future generations." It is a fundamental right of each Ugandan generation to benefit from and enjoy the natural forests and cultural patrimony inherited from previous generations in such a manner that it can be passed on to future generations in no worse condition than it was received.

The 1972 Stockholm Declaration, which first formulated this principle, states, "Man … bears a solemn responsibility to protect and improve the environment for present and future generations." President Museveni's government is obligated by international conventions to be custodian of today's environment and meet the developmental and environmental needs of present and future generations; avoid destroying Uganda's natural forests for short-term gain; and preserve for subsequent generations the use of Mabira forest.

In addressing the Mabira giveaway, it important to note the lack of any binding global treaty for the conservation and sustainable use of forests. Proposals for a convention that would regulate sustainable use of all types of forests were made during the 1992 Rio de Janeiro Conference on Environment and Development (UNCED) but were opposed by some developing countries on the grounds that this would infringe on their sovereign rights to exploit such resources.

Five texts emerged from the Rio conference. Two came from conventions, the UN Convention on Climate Change and the Convention on Biological Diversity. The third text is the "Non Legally Binding Authoritative Statement of Principles for a Global Consensus on the Management, Conservation and Sustainable Development of all Types of Forests." The last two texts are of a general nature and are the "Declaration on Environment and Development" and a program of action called Agenda 21.

The forty-chapter Agenda 21 has provisions relevant to forestry in chapter 11, whereby it details measures of dealing with all types of woodlands, forests, and forestlands, enhancing the sustainable management and conservation of all forests, and promoting efficient utilization and assessment with the aim of recovering the full valuation of goods and services by forests and forestlands.

The third text, "Nonlegally Binding Authoritative Statement of Principles for a Global Consensus on the Management, Conservation and Sustainable Development of All Types of Forests," is the first global instrument to apply to all types of forests. The text advocates the viewing of forestry issues within the context of sustainable development. It specifically calls for efforts to maintain and increase forest cover and productivity in ecological and economically sustainable ways.

Sustainable socioeconomic development is emphasized, as well as the promotion of participation of interested parties in developing national policies and outlining the rights of indigenous people. The Mabira giveaway repudiates any semblance of promoting sustainable development. It instead conjures up memories (and, some may say, current status) of the Uganda government's short-term exploitation of natural resources for private rather than public gain in the Democratic Republic of Congo (DRC).

A development path that is often exploitative socially, economically, and environmentally and benefits a small, privileged group has appropriately been termed "degenerative development."[3] The NRM government has an infamous track record of pursuing degenerative policies that will impact future generations; the exploitation of neighboring countries is a case in point.

The DRC took Uganda to the International Court of Justice (ICJ) accusing Uganda of exploiting its natural resources, including timber. The court decided in the DRC's favor, and Uganda is now obligated to pay the DRC $10 billion. Who will ultimately pay this money, if not the Ugandan taxpayer? Given the unacceptable levels of corruption and poor service delivery by the NRM government, a further burden of paying $10 billion to the DRC is unacceptable; the Ugandan people will surely demand reparation from those guilty for invading and illegally exploiting the DRC. A UN expert's report on the exploitation of DRC's natural resources also reinforces the case that the Uganda government cannot be trusted to exploit Uganda's natural resources in an economically transparent and ecologically sustainable way.

Uganda has also illegally exploited the forests of Eastern Equatoria State, in Sudan, during its Operation Iron Fist in March 2002. The operation was the UPDF's (Uganda Peoples Defence Forces) attempt to dislodge the LRA (Lord's Resistance Army) from its bases in southern Sudan. But what became evident was the traffic of UPDF trucks loaded with timber (teak) crossing the border from Sudan into Uganda. The citizens of Uganda are now wary of government initiatives that are often disguised to benefit the nation as a whole but have often only benefited a small political or military clique.

---

3   Tudela et al., 1990.

Furthermore, the Mabira giveaway violates major global conventions of which Uganda is a signatory—namely, the United Nations Convention on Climate Change, the Convention on Biological Diversity, and the Convention on International Trade in Endangered Species of Wild Fauna and Flora (CITES).

When environmentalists and other concerned citizens challenge the Mabira giveaway, they are branded "enemies of progress" by the president. What environmentalists are advocating is environmental justice in accordance with the 2003 African Convention on the Conservation of Nature and Natural Resources (Algiers Convention). Its provisions are the most comprehensive of all agreements concerning natural resources. Article III, using language from the African Charter of Human and Peoples' Rights, articulates the principle that all peoples have a right to a satisfactory environment favorable to the enjoyment of the right to development; Article XVI further complements Article III by proclaiming procedural rights and access to justice in matters related to the protection of environment and natural resources.

The convention advocates the application of the precautionary principle "with due regard to ethical and traditional values as well as scientific knowledge in the interest of present and future generations." Many concerned citizens of Uganda are urging for the application of the precautionary principle as the bare minimum in regard to the Mabira giveaway.

The president put his position on the Mabira giveaway to the Ugandan people in a *New Vision* newspaper article of April 19, 2007 that appears below, opening up further discussions on the matter. Essentially, the challenge of the present is to ensure a future.

Why I Support Mabira Forest Give-Away to Mehta Group
By Yoweri Museveni

You must have been following the controversy surrounding our decision to give some forest land to the manufacturers. There are three forest lands that have, so far, been given out to the manufacturers. These are:

- Some land in Kalangala for BIDCO, the palm oil project;
- Some forest land in Mabira for Mehta to expand his sugar operations; and
- Earlier on, we had given the planted forest at Namanve for an industrial park.

I have been involved in these land allocations. Why? It is on account of the urgent need for industrializing our very backward but rich country in terms of natural resources and raw materials. Our backwardness, at this stage, is on account of the absence of industries. In the past, our backwardness was due to many other factors: interfering with the private sector;

- Low level of literacy and education;
- Government monopolies in marketing in the form of Marketing Boards;
- A currency that was not convertible;
- Impassable roads;
- Insecurity of persons and property; etc.

The Movement has solved all these problems. To take one example, the Movement has expanded so much the education sector that we now have a very large number of university graduates floating on the streets without jobs. By 1986, Makerere University, the only university in the country at that time, used to graduate about two thousand persons each year. Today, that same Makerere graduates about ten thousand persons each year. This does not include those graduating from another seventeen universities (both government and private). How long shall we go on with this problem of educated people without jobs? This is, especially, a problem for parents who sponsor their own children. What help is the Government and the State institutions (Parliament, Civil Service, etc) giving to such parents when their children fail to get jobs after sacrificing so much to educate them through private sponsorship? How about millions of others who leave P.7, S.4 or S. 6? How can the leaders of the country take this issue in a leisurely way year after year?

Employment creation is one of my main interests when I support manufacturers, hotels, etc, in acquiring land. There are three other interests that we serve when we give manufacturers and hotels land. These are:

- Through value addition, increasing export earnings and import substitution (e.g producing sugar here instead of importing it);

- Expanding Government tax revenues because of either taxing the manufactured goods produced or (as a result of people who get jobs, while they were previously unemployed, paying indirect taxes through consumption of luxuries e.g beer, perfumes, buying expensive cars, etc – items that have taxes on them; and

- Providing markets for our raw materials produced by the farmers that just rot because of lack of processing e.g bananas, milk, etc.

The difference between Europe and, now, some of the Asian countries on the one hand and Africa on the other hand is precisely this. The others use factories to add value to their raw materials in order to get more money or even use the raw materials of those who are too uninformed to know the money lost through exporting raw materials while the Africans continue to bleed through this wrong strategy.

The problem of Africa is not lack of forests but lack of factories, hotels, real estate, professional services (e.g medical, financial, etc). UK, for instance, gets five billion pounds, through all of us using Heathrow Airport which is an example of a service industry.

Why should somebody traveling to America (North or South) go through London or Paris? Why not use Dakar? Look at the map. He / she does so because there are facilities at Heathrow that are not at Dakar. Previously agricultural land at Heathrow was converted into a modern airport. Those 1,391 acres that Heathrow occupies would not earn the UK five billion pounds, if they were still agricultural.

We therefore, need to balance the needs of preserving the eco-system with the needs for social transformation – changing the society from peasant to middle class, skilled working class society. This means that the majority of the people should shift from agriculture to industries and services. Having too many people in agriculture as we do now (82%), is one of the characteristics of backwardness. Countries like UK (population fifty-six million) or USA (population three hundred million) services have got only 2% of their population in agriculture respectively. The rest are in industries or services. Even newly industrialized countries like Taiwan, South Korea, Malaysia, or Thailand, the portions of their populations which are still in agriculture are: 6%, 6.4%, 14.5%, and 49% respectively. This is why their societies are more prosperous than ours. Some of these countries used to produce some agricultural raw materials such as silk, tea, (e.g Japan) or palm oil (e.g Malaysia). Today, they either no longer do so or they are reducing the acreage under those crops. They have converted that land to industries and services. The gap between the industrialized countries and our backward countries, as I have told you many times, is big because industrial products fetch more money than raw materials.

Take the example of our own coffee. A kilogram of unprocessed coffee will bring US $1, while that same kg will fetch US $15 when it is processed in the Nestle factories in UK. Who, then, is aiding who? It is the same story for cotton. Failure to see this, yet we are in leadership of Africa today, is nothing short of treason. Our ignorant traditional chiefs caused our enslavement in the past; ignorant African elite are responsible for our continued enslavement today.

Let us, again, take one other example of employment. Madhvani at Kakira employs about six thousand five hundred persons. Suppose we had two thousand Madhvanis, we would be able to employ thirteen million people. The level of unemployment would be much less in Uganda. We would have to import labour from other countries like Japan does. People from other countries would be coming here for kyeyo. Therefore, obstructing investors or demonizing them as the pro-enemy press (The Monitor) is doing is, indeed, an enemy act – an act by those that do not want Uganda to transition from backwardness to modernity!

Why, then, use forest lands? This is because there is no free land. Much of the land is occupied by peasants who are engaged in traditional, subsistence farming. Both physically and legally we cannot access land. However, I have instructed Uganda Investment Authority (UIA) to slowly buying land in order to create a Land Bank for this purpose; but this is a slow process. We cannot wait for it. Otherwise, we shall lose opportunities which will be taken up by others. The king of business is the consumer – the one who buys from you. If you disappoint him, especially in export markets where there are many competitors, he will never buy from you again. This is why I have been using Government lands to fill this gap. I converted Namanve into an industrial park. When it is finished, it will accommodate about one thousand factories. One hundred seventy six (176) factories and enterprises have already applied for land there. Namanve will be a satellite town of Kampala. There is already the Coca-Cola factory there, in that area. It is already employing seven hundred persons. Therefore, these one thousand factories could employ seven hundred thousand persons. I used part of the prison land at Luzira. Already seventeen factories and enterprises have already been allocated that land! What a wastage it was to have 480 acres just being used by convicts to grow sweet potatoes (only sixty-two acres were given to UIA to allocate to the investors). How much does an acre of sweet potatoes bring in? How much money would the sixty-two acres of sweet potatoes bring in? How much will the seventeen enterprises now going to use the Luzira land going to bring in? How many Ugandans will be employed there? It is the answers to these rhetorical questions that guide my actions.

Then we have got potential goldmine – BIDCO. Uganda imports cooking oil and tallow (for making soap) worth US $47.7m per year. Palm trees are some of the source for these vegetable oils. The East African market for vegetable oil is worth US $700m. This chance came to us because Malaysia, on account of industrialization, no longer has land for growing palm plantations. Palm trees can only grow in lands that receive rainfalls of about 2,000 mm per annum. There are only a few areas like that in East Africa including Ssese Islands and Bundibugyo. I could not miss such a chance for my country. I ordered the responsible people to get 6,500 hectares (3,000 hectares was public land under the district and three thousand five hundred was bought by the Government for BIDCO). However, for the factory at Jinja to make profit, they need palm oil from 10,000 hectares of land. The only other land was the forest land nearby. Palm trees are, indeed, a forest. They are trees that both capture carbon dioxide from the atmosphere for photo synthesis but also make money for the country and create employment. How can we miss such an opportunity? BIDCO activities have already transformed Kalangala. When I went there last year, people at Bukakata told me that there was now traffic "jammo" at the ferry because of the increased activities. Why should any Ugandan obstruct, harangue or inconvenience such people? What sort of disorientation is this? How can enemies of the future of the people of Uganda be allowed to thrive? Our newspaper such as The Monitor are ever scaring away such investors—such allies of our children's future. The delays and controversies generated by the enemies of progress and permitted to continue make us lose opportunities.

In respect of Mehta, as you know, he has been producing sugar for Uganda for a long time. Amin destroyed their production in 1972. By destroying our entrepreneurs, Amin destroyed the small nucleus of the modern economy of Uganda. That is how we got into a lot of shortages and got left behind by other countries like South Korea, Singapore, Malaysia, Thailand, etc. When we came into Government, we brought these entrepreneurs back. Many of them have already attained their 1972 levels and even surpassed them. They are now facing new challenges. One of them is the challenge of competition from China, India and other developing countries. Our industries must be assisted to be competitive by lowering costs of production so that they can sell at lower prices and, therefore, capture international markets. One way of lowering costs is to increase production so that the producer benefits from the economies of large-scale production.

For example, once I have used Uganda shillings twenty million to build a dip-tank for my cattle, it will be more economical to dip two thousand cattle through that facility per week rather than just one hundred per week. This is, therefore, the same story with the sugar factories. According to Mehta, in order to be competitive, he should go from his present level of 55,000 tonnes per annum to 110,000 tonnes per annum. In order to do that he needs 1.2m tonnes of sugarcane per annum, which can only be produced on 22,500 hectares of usable land. He now has 10,000 hectares under sugar cane. Therefore, he needs an extra seven thousand one hundred hectares from Government; he wants to buy 1,500 hectares from private people and the out growers will supply him with 60,000 tonnes of sugar cane. We cannot shift the factory and the present 10,000 hectares of sugarcane. When Mehta brought the proposal of the forest land, I supported the idea without hesitation. I request you to, similarly, support the idea. Why?

First of all, for the reasons I have already enumerated above: employment creation, export earnings or import savings, tax revenues for the Government, etc. In addition, however, by-products of sugar can be used to generate electricity and to make fuel that can be mixed in petroleum as they do in Brazil. Therefore, a sugar cane plantation is also an oilfield like the ones we recently discovered in Lake Albert because they can produce bio-fuel.

However, there are forests we should not compromise about. The forests next to the Lake should never be touched. Some 50–200 metres of forest belt next to the lake should never be touched because it helps to filter the water flowing into the lake so that it does not carry soil silt into the lake. The so-called "environmentalists" never talk about this. Fifty metres of forest next to river banks should never be touched. That is how soil is washed into the river bed causing silting, for example, in Lake Kyoga, causing swamp grass to swallow the white water (open water) portion. Hills and hill-tops could also be saved to avoid soil erosion. Wetlands should never be touched because these are the water reservoirs for our country; those that have been encroached on should be bought back at attractive prices. We should plant forests on all the bare hills of Rwampara, Ssingo, Kabale, Karamoja, Akokoro, etc. These hills, with a high gradient, are not good for crops. They can, however, be used for certain species of trees: eucalyptus, black wattle (burikoote), carriandra, etc. We shall end up with forests, more factories, more employment, etc. Some of the opposition and their press are envious of our achievements. They are worried that if we implement what we have planned, they will be marginalized forever. Hence their opposition, we should not be fooled.

Finally, I would like to unequivocally assert that it is more difficult for a backward country to guard against environmental degradation "than for a camel to go through the eye of a needle." Why? It is because of the following reasons:

- The Government has no money to police and protect the environment;
- There are too many people, in primitive agriculture who, in the process, destroy the environment using wrong techniques and implements;
- Without electricity, the population uses firewood, thereby destroying the bio-mass.

Therefore, industrialization is a sine qua non of protecting the environment. There are some who do not protect the environment even after industrialization. That is not because of lack of means but because of greed which is a different problem. In our case, the environment (especially the forests and bio-mass) are being destroyed because of lack of industrialization and the attendant social transformation. Europeans and the Americans are destroying the environment because of greed; we are destroying the environment, involuntarily, because of poverty, lack of employment, lack of electricity, etc.

The Banyankole say, "*kandide ehweyo achmita omukira*"—the one who wants the whole animal to expose itself for better targeting ends up only injuring the tail of the animal and not killing it. Even the English say, "Procrastination is the thief to time." Mistakes by the Sixth Parliament caused the present power shortage. The mistake of the so-called donors in constraining our defense expenditure (limiting it, arbitrarily, to 2 percent of GDP) caused the prolonging of the Kony war until 2002, when we firmly rejected their meddling—that is how we defeated Kony and we are now ending the cattle rustling in Karamoja. I request you to support our move on these limited portions of our forest reserves that are not part of the core ecosystems mentioned above (next to rivers, next to lake shores, wetlands, forests on mountain tops, etc.), which must be preserved at all costs.

Chapter 2

PRECAUTIONARY PRINCIPLE

*It is our task in our time and in our generation to
hand down undiminished to those who come after us,
as was handed down to us by those who went before the
natural wealth and beauty which is ours.*

**John F. Kennedy,
in a speech dedicating the National Wildlife Federation
Building on March 3, 1961**

How should Uganda think about worst-case scenarios resulting from deforestation? Is there a framework that may be utilized to address a worst-case scenario? The precautionary principle now used in many international conventions and declarations is often cited as a possible answer. Consider a few examples:

(1)   The 1992 Rio Declaration's Principle 15 proclaims, "In order to protect the environment, the precautionary principle shall be widely applied by States according to their capabilities. Where there are threats of serious or irreversible damage, lack of full scientific certainty shall not be used as a reason for postponing cost-effective measures to prevent environmental degradation."

(2)   The United Nations Framework Convention on Climate Change declares, "Where there are threats of serious or irreversible damage, lack of full scientific certainty should not be used as a reason for postponing [regulatory] measures, taking into account that policies and measures to deal with climate change should be cost-effective so as to ensure global benefits at the lowest possible cost."

(3)   The European Communication on Precautionary Principle (EU, 2000) states, "The precautionary principle applies where scientific evidence is insufficient, inconclusive or uncertain and preliminary scientific evaluation indicates that there are reasonable grounds for concern that the potentially dangerous effects on the environment, human, animal or plant health may be inconsistent with the high level of protection chosen by the EU."

Whatever way the precautionary principle is formulated, at its core lie worst-case scenarios and the threat of catastrophic harm. Essentially, the precautionary principle has shifted discussion from postdamage control (civil liability as a curative tool) to deliberations on predamage control (anticipatory measures) of risks. The precautionary principle is often seen as an integral principle of sustainable development. Regardless of the different definitions, some common elements can be discerned:

-   A wait-and-see strategy is not an option. Interventions are required before possible harm occurs.
-   The principle applies when there exist considerable scientific uncertainties about the nature, probability, and magnitude of harm.
-   To trigger the principle, some form of scientific analysis is required.
-   Value-laden language that expresses a moral judgment about acceptability of the possible harm is included.

Environmentalists in Uganda recognize that in order to trigger the precautionary principle, the grounds for concern need to be plausible and/

or tenable. Ugandans know that forest destruction is harmful, and this is consistent with current knowledge and ecological theories. This position is plausible and in accordance with widely accepted scientific theories and facts. Plausibility does not need to be correlated with probability, and the two concepts should not be confused.

When opponents of the Mabira giveaway hold the hypothesis that the destruction of part of Mabira will cause catastrophic harm, they are in fact stating that this plausible hypothesis is more probable with the position held by President Museveni; what they are saying is that their plausible hypothesis is more of a possibility with irreversible consequences if the government continues to pursue short-term growth through a nineteenth-century industrialization model advocated by the Ugandan president.

The president fears the application of the precautionary approach, as it may stifle the quick-profit route followed by the military elite and government cronies, most evidently in the exploitation of natural resources of the DRC. Furthermore, the development path espoused by the president is based on the simple science and the economics of the first industrial revolution. The president calls opponents of the giveaway "enemies of progress," and yet wider use of the precautionary principle can help stimulate both modern economic innovation and science, replacing nineteenth-century industrialization technologies with the clean technologies and systems of a new twenty-first-century industrial revolution.

It is important to point out that the application of the precautionary principle does not eliminate all risks but aims to achieve lower or more acceptable risks or hazards than are likely to occur if part of the Mabira forest is given to Mehta. The principle is based on a rational-decision rule and aims to use the best systems sciences of complex processes so as to make wiser development decisions. In using systems sciences, it is crucial to look at the scientific and legal concepts and techniques used to safeguard biological diversity (or biodiversity).

It is unfortunate that precautionary programs to mitigate the adverse effects of environmental degradation and curb global warming have not been pursued, and the effects are now evident—for example, most of the ice on the Rwenzori Mountains between Uganda and Congo has gone. The effects are regional, for 80 percent of the ice on Mount Kilimanjaro has melted away in a span of ninety years, and of the eighteen glaciers on Mount Kenya, seven have already been lost. Global warming is real; 1998 was the warmest year of the twentieth century, and East Africa saw the worst floods for half a century in 1997 and 1998. There is growing evidence that weather phenomena like El Niños and El Niñas are becoming stronger and more frequent due to global warming.

In 2007, the International Climate Risk Report pointed out that Uganda is one of the most vulnerable and least prepared to deal with climate change. Notable scholars such as Professor G. W. Otim-Nape and Dr. Kitara David-Lagoro have publicly come out to highlight that climate change is a serious issue. Some initiatives have addressed this climate issue, such as the "Adaptation to the Impact of Climate Variability on Food and Health Security in the Cattle Corridor of Uganda" project. This program is being led by Africa Innovations Institute (AII), which received Ushs 1.2 billion from the International Development Research Centre (IDRC). This is commendable, but not enough.

Environmentalists in Uganda advocate the precautionary principle as a safeguard not only to the environment, but to Ugandans alive today and succeeding generations. The people of Uganda have no confidence in the government's capacity to offer post-disaster relief, rehabilitation, and reconstruction programs. This became clear after the mudslides disaster in Bududa District on March 2, 2010. The painful part of this story is that this disaster was predicted, and some actions could have been undertaken to address it. Landslides are an emerging issue, and the NEMA State of Environment Report (2008) identified eleven areas of concern, including Bududa.

A wait-and-see approach by the government goes against the very concept of the precautionary principle, which urges anticipatory measures. Uganda's meteorologists have been issuing warnings of an impending weather calamity since the middle of 2009. In August 2009, Uganda's commissioner for meteorology Stephen Magezi urged the government to start preparing for heavy rains. He pointed out that there was a 70 percent chance of heavy, destructive rains that would affect around 10 percent of the population in the west, east, and southern parts of the country.

What is even more alarming regarding the government's lack of emergency preparedness in 2010 is that the El Niño rains of 2007 (for which the government was not prepared), which led to flooding in the Teso and Lango subregions, led to loss of life, destruction of livelihoods, and the displacement of an estimated three hundred thousand people. One would think that the government would have learned from this experience and be better prepared in the future. Instead, in September 2009, the people of Uganda were lied to by the then Relief and Disaster Minister Tarsis Kabwegyere: "We are now better prepared to handle the situation than we were in 2007." This is far from the truth, according to the State of Environment Report (2008), which states unequivocally that, "in the case of Uganda, the Department of Disaster Preparedness is very ill prepared and is short on institutional capacity."

The human tragedies in Uganda are indicative of the serious policy deficits and mismanagement by the NRM leadership. In spite of warnings from Stephen Magezi about seasonal variations "becoming more frequent and severe … because of climate change," the citizens are lied to, and it is business as usual. Has the NRM government no conscience? Has the leadership made a moral judgment about the acceptability of the possible harm to its citizens through environmental degradation?

Environmental damage can be irreversible, and even when it is not, the Uganda government cannot be relied upon to make amends. Despite ample warnings, the response to the Bududa landslide was unacceptable; a responsive, caring government would have sacked the disaster minister.

Ugandans now know that their government cannot handle environmental disasters. Precaution is the only way forward.

Just to highlight the lies and incompetencies, note that in 2009, Commissioner for Disaster Preparedness Martin Owor insisted that his ministry was ready for any weather-related emergencies that might occur. The *Saturday Monitor* newspaper quotes him as saying, "We don't sit back and wait, we always take action in preparation of El Niño," but he goes on to state that measures to address a disaster are preliminary. This is contradictory: Are we ready, or are only preliminary processes under way to make the ministry ready?

Former Finance Minister Syda Bbumba is also on record saying that her ministry does not put money aside for the predicted floods, because there is no certainty that they will occur—in spite of science-based predictions from the meteorology department that there was a 70 percent chance of heavy rains. The *Saturday Monitor* quotes her as saying, "we don't give money for disasters in advance."

When disaster strikes in Uganda, ad hoc mechanisms kick in whereby individual ministries appeal to the Ministry of Finance for funds to address the crisis if they do not have enough money in their existing budgets. So, in order to address a crisis, the ministry has to withdraw funds from existing programs to fund an emergency or trundle through the bureaucratic minefield to secure funds for disaster relief while the disaster unfolds. It would, however, be unfair to paint all ministries with the same brush; some, like the Ministry of Health, have emergency measures in place at all times, regardless of whether a heavy rain forecast has been given.

Climate-related disasters in Uganda contribute to over 70 percent of natural disasters and destroy an average of 800,000 hectares of crops annually, making losses in excess of Ushs 120 billion. Economic losses resulting from the outbreak of disease, destroyed transport, and damage to the economic infrastructure are estimated at well over UShs 50 billion. The evidence is clear that any development path that destroys the environment in the long run is not development at all, but backwardness.

And when disaster strikes? The victims are to blame. After the Bududa District landslide, President Museveni toured the affected areas wearing military fatigues and carrying an AK-47 while blaming the people for living on and cultivating on the slopes of Mount Elgon. Yes, it seems hard to believe, but this is true. The uncomfortable fact is that the political leadership behaves as if they are totally ignorant of the real socioeconomic situations in the country; when the president blames the victims of a disaster while the ministry that should have taken the lead in coordinating the disaster response is caught unprepared despite early warning memos from the meteorology department, what are we to make of the current government?

Of course, preventive measures like preserving forests and planting trees are preferable to dealing with the aftermath of a disaster. The Bududa disaster is indicative of the bankruptcy of the NRM leadership that, through bad governance, has undermined the efforts of institutions such as the Uganda Wildlife Authority, the National Forestry Authority, and the National Environment Management Authority to carry out their mandates to protect our environment and support sustainable agricultural practices.

The president himself in the past stopped the National Forest Authority from evicting people who had illegally encroached on forest reserves. Furthermore, the government has not employed or enforced safer settlement and agricultural practices as a means of preventing environmental degradation and weather-related disasters. In fact, government has been impeding some of the institutions mentioned above from actually empowering communities to look after their environments and develop community coping mechanisms.

It is indeed a great shame for Africa when the president of Uganda, who is supposedly retired from the army, dons a military uniform to visit the victims of a disaster that could have been prevented if appropriate environmental programs had been implemented. His insulting of his people only goes to show that the current Uganda leadership has neither learned to assume responsibility for the management of the country nor learned from similar past experiences.

Climate variations are not new phenomena. For example, periods of drought can be traced back several centuries, and from 1800 to 1900 droughts occurred at least every twenty years. But recent trends indicate that the intervals are becoming shorter as a result of environmental degradation. But what is interesting is that in the past, communities had coping mechanisms to deal with drought without it leading to famine.

Clearly, in the twenty-first century, countries like Uganda should be able to deal with environmental variations without it turning into a disaster. But like many African countries, Uganda has adopted development models that have played down the importance of agricultural production while giving prominence to cash crops at the expense of food crops. Failure to modify this development model has exposed the rural people to the vagaries of weather; this is further exacerbated by corruption, which leads to bad governance.

It is for this reason that a precautionary approach to environmental protection and development is of paramount importance. Prevention is better than a cure, particularly when the doctor administering the cure does not possess the will or aptitude to heal the patient. Although I have digressed a little from talking about the Mabira, I think the point is clear: If we let disasters happen, President Museveni will only shift the blame to the victims.

What is particularly alarming is the realization that the government takes no responsibility for the environment despite being a signatory to a number of environmental conventions. This fact dawned on me while listening to a radio program, "Hot Seat," on Kiss FM. The show, which aired on March 3, 2010, addressed the government's response to the Bududa landslide.

The show featured the Minister of Information and National Guidance Kabakumba Masiko and the chairman of Parliament's Public Accounts Committee, Nandala Mafabi.

At one point, regarding the relief response, the minister said, "Red Cross is down there and among other things, they have contributed tarpaulins, and you don't expect the government to do that." Ms. Minister, *yes*, the people of Uganda do expect the government to lead the disaster response, with the Red Cross and other agencies in support. Unlike other NGOs, the Uganda Red Cross Society was created by an act of Parliament (The Red Cross Act No. 23 of 1964). Its roles and responsibilities are well defined as an auxiliary to government. Furthermore, the National Policy for Internally Displaced Persons states that the minister of disaster preparedness and refugees is charged with overall responsibility for all matters relating to internally displaced persons. Mafabi also asked about the Ushs 4 billion contingency fund; no adequate answer was given by the minister, who then accused him of making political capital out of the disaster.

In hindsight, Masiko is probably right: The people of Uganda no longer expect much from the NRM government—hence the demonstration on the Mabira giveaway in the first place.

The tragedy that unfolded in Bududa in March 2010 is a culmination of global warming, monoculture agriculture, bad governance, and a total disregard for early warnings from meteorologists. Kevin Trenberth, head of climate analysis at the National Center for Atmospheric Research (NCAR) in Boulder, Colorado, in the United States, is one of the first researchers to link the recent strong and increasingly frequent El Niños to the hand of man.

El Niños are redistributors of heat and energy in the hottest part of the world's oceans; they take place when the regular circulation systems cannot cope. It would now appear that because of so much warming in the tropical Pacific, the usual pattern of occasional El Niños to distribute heat are no longer adequate.

Scientists are still developing a full understanding of the El Niño enigma, and many unanswered questions remain. But enough is known to ascertain that it is a phenomenon that transfers heat and moisture in massive amounts around the tropics. Enough is known about it to predict when it will drop by and probable impact on communities.

So if global warming is a factor behind the recent spate of violent El Niños, what can Uganda do? For one thing, we should preserve our forests, as carbon sinks. Uganda needs to follow a development path that is cognizant of the precautionary principle rather than following economic policies that lead to disasters that the country is unable to cope with.

When government diverts funds from development projects to deal with the aftermath of weather-related disasters that often amount to destroyed livelihoods, what starts off as a short-term relief exercise ends up being more permanent. It is well known that around the world, one can find "temporary" settlements that have been around for over two decades. Some of the victims of the 2007 floods that destroyed food crops and led to drought have yet to recover from that tragedy. Uganda is still an exporter of raw materials, mainly coffee—this important cash crop has also been affected by climate change, and yields are down. In whatever development model the NRM government pursues, it cannot afford to ignore the environment. A developmental path devoid of environmental concerns is a dysfunctional and degenerative one.

Environmentalists are not enemies of progress, but advocates of good governance. It is clear that Uganda cannot continue as is. A paradigm shift in developmental thinking has got to take place at the policy level. What happened in Bududa is the sort of worst-case scenario that the precautionary principle aims to avoid.

The development path the president is advocating is virtually unchanged from the one that the colonial authorities pursued in Uganda in the 1940s. The 1949 Development Plan for Uganda stated,

> The development of some industries, especially those for
> processing primary products, is of great importance, not
> so much in the increase of wealth which will result, as in
> providing one of the main stimulants to the development
> of an internal economy ... It is in the establishment of
> such secondary industries that private enterprise can make
> its greatest contribution to development.

The president ignores the environmentalists and climate change at his own peril. Uganda had an IDP population of up to two million people due to a counterinsurgency strategy in northern Uganda—a conflict that went on for two decades, although it has abated at the time of writing. The government forced, with scarce attention to international law, entire communities into camps rather than protect them from the LRA; this violates international human rights law and humanitarian standards. In July 2005 a joint Ministry of Health and World Health Organization (WHO) report, "Health and mortality survey among internally displaced persons in Gulu, Kitgum and Pader, northern Uganda," noted in its main findings that almost one thousand excess deaths per week were occurring through government neglect, resulting in starvation, dehydration, and deaths through treatable diseases. By and large, the government has managed to contain dissent among the victims of war. But can the government contain dissent from what are now commonly termed "climate refugees" all over Uganda?

Precautionary approaches may also save Museveni's presidency and legacy. Haile Selassie of Ethiopia ignored early warning reports of looming drought from 1972–1973. Failure to address this led to famine and to a military coup that removed him from power in 1974. Uganda has managed to avoid famine but needs to consider the environment in present and future economic-development programs. Like the environment, Uganda's economy is fragile and very reliant on a stable climate; adverse climate shocks could have political and social consequences that Uganda does not need.

Chapter 3

BIOLOGICAL DIVERSITY

*The nation behaves well if it treats the national
resources as assets which it must turn over to the next
generation increased, and not impaired, in value.*

Theodore Roosevelt,
in a speech to the Colorado Livestock Association,
August 29, 1910

The Mabira tropical forest is an interesting and complex natural system covering approximately 29,964 hectares; it hosts numerous trees, birds, and butterfly species, and it is a water-catchment area for the Lake Victoria and Lake Kyoga basins. It also has significant cultural importance to the Baganda, who believe the forest is the home of the gods of rain and food.

In order to understand the potential harmful effects on the Mabira forest, one needs to look at the new scientific theory of change called chaos theory. This theory elucidates how natural systems, such as tropical forests, show significant changes in the way they interact within an ecosystem while remaining in the same overall pattern ("dynamic equilibrium").[4]

---

4 Discussion of chaos theory from *Earth in the Balance* by Al Gore.

This theory points out that certain critical boundaries define a dynamic equilibrium position. If these limits are exceeded, equilibrium is threatened. Large changes, such as the giving away of one-fourth of Mabira, may suddenly affect these boundaries, thereby shifting the entire regional ecosystem into a different and possibly unsustainable equilibrium.

Former US vice president and Nobel laureate Al Gore, in his book *Earth in the Balance*, points out that the relationship between human civilization and the earth is now in a state that theorists of change would describe as disequilibrium. He goes on to quote Albert Einstein at the dawn of the nuclear age: "Everything has changed but our way of thinking." He further points out that at the birth of the environmental age, the same point holds.

In Uganda, the understanding of and approach to ecology, ecosystems, and human development lag behind the conventional wisdom. The president reduces environmental concerns to silting, erosion, and the artificial reconstitution of ecosystems (plant forest on all bare hills), referring to concerned citizens as "so-called environmentalists," missing the point altogether. The "so-called environmentalists" are, yes, concerned about erosion and silting, but they are also concerned with the unique biodiversity of the forest at three levels: genetic, species, and ecosystem.

Uganda is a signatory to the 1992 Convention on Biological Diversity (CBD), which describes biological diversity as "the variability among living organisms from all sources including, inter alia, terrestrial, marine and other aquatic ecosystems and the ecological complexes of which they are part; this includes diversity within species, between species and of ecosystems" (Article 2).

Under the CBD, Uganda is obligated to conserve biological diversity for a number of reasons, which I have outlined below.

Scientific reasons: It is prudent to conserve Mabira for its enormous "library" of scientific information. Far too little is known about the unique ensemble of proteins; enzymes; hormones; other organic substances; physiological, ecological, and behavioral processes; and genes of species found in the forest. No one knows which of these might one day prove to be of scientific importance for mankind.

It is of paramount importance that as many species as possible are saved for breakthroughs in agriculture and medicine. Agriculture depends on new varieties of crops from the wild gene stock available, from which, through biotechnology, we are able to cultivate improved strains. The discovery of new species or attributes of old ones hitherto unknown could benefit mankind. For example, it was relatively recently that scientists discovered that the only animal other than man capable of contracting leprosy is the armadillo; this information has led to the work on a vaccine for the disease.

The Baganda, along with other less dominant tribes, are already using the Mabira forest for medicinal purposes. Many medicines are of natural origin, either extracted directly from wild species or synthesized on the basis of molecules discovered in these species. These include aspirin, morphine, digitalin, and quinine. Cyclosporin is an important and powerful immunodepressant used in organ-transplant operations, and it is produced from a microscopic fungus. Traditional medicine has yet to be studied in depth; further research on species and ecosystems will undoubtedly help in developing practical applications and appropriate intellectual property that can benefit Ugandans and mankind as a whole.

Economic reasons: The Mabira forest receives more than 62 percent of the tourist traffic to forest reserves in Uganda. The ecotourism sector is also the second largest foreign-exchange earner; therefore preserving Mabira makes economic sense. Ecotourism is environmentally friendly and sustainable, whereas single-crop plantation agriculture has proven to be environmentally destructive. Tourism and forestry are some of the primary growth areas of the National Development Plan. And in 2008, according to the World Tourism and Travel Council, tourism contributed 9.2 percent, or US $1.2 billion, of Uganda's gross domestic product (GDP).

It is imperative to challenge the mind-set of decision makers and change their concept of economic development and our relationship to the environment. Following events described by chaos theory, it is possible that little changes like destroying parts of Mabira may lead to environmental thresholds being passed, and then a cascade of dramatic changes will occur all at once.

One of the questions environmentalists are concerned about is this: Who gains from the sale of logs from the forest? This question was ignored by the president in his printed defense of the giveaway. Ugandans are cognizant of patterns of abusive exploitation of timber and other natural resources in the DRC for quick economic gain by criminal networks involving Ugandan military officers, as outlined in a United Nations report.[5]

Two issues come to the fore. First, the president attempts to highlight the difference between developed and developing countries by saying that the developed countries "use factories to add value to their raw materials in order to get more money or even use the raw materials of those who are too uninformed to know the money lost through exporting raw materials while Africans continue to bleed through this wrong strategy."

It is therefore appropriate to ask again: Who will gain from the sale of timber from Mabira if land is cleared for sugar plantations? Will timber be exported? Will value-added activity take place in Uganda? Why is nothing mentioned about the timber that will be lost from Mabira? When Uganda invaded eastern Congo and began exploiting natural resources of DRC, no value-added activity took place in Uganda. This led to the term "warehouse state," whereby raw materials merely transited through Uganda to other parts of the world. More important, cutting down trees and selling the lumber for income places no value on the depreciation of the Mabira forest. The gains of the Mabira giveaway may actually be an illusion based on a failure to account adequately for reduction in natural capital.

---

5   Expert Panel Report on exploitation of natural resources (DRC).

As long as biological resources remain invisible (in economic terms), underpriced, or unpriced, decision makers will inevitably gravitate toward short-term gains from resource exploitation for economic gain against the long-term benefit of conserving natural resources. Biological resources hold the promise of new products. Rubber and quinine both came from the discovery of new trees; new products of equal importance may be waiting to be discovered, but only if we take the long view.

The second issue is corruption, which will be discussed in more detail later. Nevertheless, it is important to note that the pervasiveness of corruption is an environmental and ecological problem. Corruption lessens transparency and accountability, on which democratic government—and the public's ability to share stewardship of the environment—depend.

An area of twenty-first-century economic development can be found in the field of gene technology. It is well known within the scientific community that it is not always necessary (and indeed, in some cases may not be possible) to cultivate wild plants for their genetic properties. The immense economic possibilities of employing methods of identifying and isolating genes for manufacture *in situ* should not be ignored.

It is clear that biological diversity is not a major concern of the president, even though biodiversity was recognized as a fundamental value for mankind at the 1972 Conference on the Human Environment in Stockholm, which adopted an action plan comprising 109 recommendations and a Declaration of Principles for the Preservation and Enhancement of the Human Environment: "The natural resources of the earth including the air, water, land, flora and fauna and especially representative samples of natural ecosystems must be safeguarded for the benefit of present and future generations through careful planning or management, as appropriate" (Principle 2).

It should be recognized that the Stockholm principles are not legally binding; they take the form of soft law, which does not require the government of Uganda to make formal legal commitments. However, these principles have since been developed further by the 1982 World Charter for Nature and the 1992 Rio Declaration on Environment and Development, accelerating consensus and the development of hard (legally binding) law.

Opponents of the Mabira giveaway are aware that, following the Stockholm Conference, a number of environmental treaties of which Uganda is a signatory were limited in scope to species or sectors—for example, CITES, whereby species not expressly covered by the treaty do not benefit from protection. Nevertheless, a rapid legal evolution and paradigm shift in thinking about the environment in Uganda, championed by NGOs, has gradually brought national and international attention to the need for an inclusive approach to conserving biodiversity.

Biological diversity conservation has three major goals:

- maintenance of essential ecological processes;
- preservation of genetic diversity (i.e., biological diversity); and
- sustainable use of species and ecosystems.

The above goals buttress the 1992 Convention on Biological Diversity. Some negotiators at the Rio conference wanted biodiversity designated as a common heritage of mankind.[6] However, the concept of common heritage has raised significant controversies, and conflicting understandings of its substance and content has led to it being rejected for another derivative: "common concern of mankind."

The "common concern of mankind" concept is particularly apt in addressing the negative impact of forest destruction in East Africa through two important templates: temporal and spatial. The spatial aspects mean that common concern implies cooperation of all states in the Great Lakes region in particular because of the influence on regional weather by tropical rain

---

6   The heritage concept affirmed in the Stockholm Declaration is reflected in a few treaties, notably the 1972 World Heritage Convention.

forests. The temporal aspect arises from major environmental challenges, implications, and impacts over the long term, which affect the rights and obligations not only of present population, but also of future generations.

Uganda's illegal exploitation of lumber in DRC and the Mabira giveaway both ignore the common concern of the region, given the scientific evidence and knowledge on the relationship between forests and the earth's water system. First, forest destruction can affect the hydrological cycle (the natural water-distribution system) in a given area. Merely banning the destruction of some 50–200 meters of forest belt next to lakes like Victoria and Kyoga, as the president wants, misses the point completely.

Why? Well, for starters, a considerable amount of water is stored in the forests of the earth—especially tropical rain forests such as Mabira. Forests themselves produce rain clouds through evapotranspiration and evaporation from surfaces like broad leaves. Forests may also attract rain by emitting gases called terpenes, as well as a chemical called dimethylsulfide, both of which are released into the atmosphere by forests, whereby they undergo oxidation and transform into a sulfate. Droplets of rainwater coalesce around these sulfate particles.

The science and relationship between rain and forests is still being studied, but what is irrefutable is when forests are destroyed, rainfall reduces. Evidence of this can be found in Ethiopia whereby forested land decreased from 40 percent to 1 percent over the last four decades,[7] this has resulted in a drastic fall in rainfall leading to prolonged periods of drought.

Lake Victoria, the largest freshwater lake in Africa, is mainly rain-fed and has catchment areas composed of wetlands, forests, and several tributaries throughout the Lake Victoria basin. The lake is an important natural resource to a number of states, including Kenya, Rwanda, Burundi, Sudan, Tanzania, and the DRC. What is alarming is that Lake Victoria's water levels have fallen drastically and may continue to do so. The president talks about building factories and industrialization. How can factories run without energy?

---

7   Al Gore

At the time of writing, Uganda is experiencing an energy crisis characterized by insufficient water supply for industrial use and energy generation. This crisis is marked by electricity shortages, blackouts, brownouts, and load shedding. As water levels continue to fall in Lake Victoria, building factories reminiscent of nineteenth-century industrialization will remain a pipe dream. Recent studies have shown that inappropriate policies by government leading to the over-release of water through the power stations at Jinja is the main cause of falling water levels.

Any industrialization strategy for Uganda or the region must be cognizant of the importance and role of Lake Victoria, the River Nile, hydroelectric power generation, and technological advancements in clean and renewable energy sources such as wind and solar technology. The current industrial policy carries too high an environmental price for it to be sustainable. Even in Brazil, a country the president wants to emulate, deforestation is a concern for it is responsible for 80 percent of Brazil's carbon-dioxide emissions. Biofuel production is only suitable where the overall effect is positive. For example, a biofuel using household organic waste, such as matoke peels harvested at household level, goes a longer way than destroying our natural and cultural heritage in pursuit of the profit motive.

The president states that byproducts of sugar can be used to generate electricity. This is absurd, to say the least, for any energy-generating benefits of planting sugar in Mabira have got to be weighed against other alternatives, such as hydroelectricity. The DRC has the potential to supply electricity to the entire Great Lakes region. The Congo River with a volume of 30,000 to 60,000 cubic meters per second could potentially supply 600 billion kilowatt hours annually. The environmental cost of destroying the forest will lead to climate change for Mabira, one of Uganda's largest carbon sinks. Losing Mabira would greatly increase carbon emissions and contribute to global warming. Under the Climate Change Convention, Uganda should reduce its carbon footprint. Furthermore, sugarcane production is likely to reduce organic carbon and other nutrients in the soil, creating a need for artificial fertilizers.

The Uganda government refutes this claim and asserts that the main cause of the decline of the Lake Victoria water levels is drought. If this is the case, why does the president want to follow a policy of forest degradation that will affect the hydrological cycle and lead to more drought—which will then impact rainfall and consequently rain-fed lakes like Lake Victoria? The prospects of drought and over-release of water at the power plants does not augur well for the future of Uganda, and biofuels from sugar are not capable of solving the energy crisis.

The Owens Falls Dam (renamed Nalubaale) was designed to generate hydroelectric power without disrupting the natural flow of the water from the lake. In order to achieve this, a formula known as the Agreed Curve was set to govern the water flow through the dam. This formula designates the maximum water flow of between 300 cubic meters and 1,700 cubic meters per second, depending on the water level in the lake.

Experts have said that Uganda's energy problems began in 2002, after the completion of the Kiira hydroelectric power complex in Jinja, which created a second outlet at a lower gradient than the natural barrier. A hydrologist with the United Nations International Strategy for Disaster, Daniel Kull, estimated that in the period of 2003–2004, the two Ugandan dams (Owens and Kiira) have released water at an average of almost 1,250 cubic meters per second—55 percent more than was permitted at the given water levels.

The president requested the support of Ugandans to "move on these limited portions of our forest reserves that are not part of the core ecosystems," which he believes are limited to forests next to rivers and lake shores, on mountains, and in wetlands. This viewpoint shows a lack of understanding of the holistic interconnectedness of genetic, species, and ecosystem diversity. One cannot be a little pregnant; either you are or are not; you either have a viable ecosystem or not; a move on these limited portions is in fact a move to destroy the ecosystem; trying to differentiate between what constitutes part of a "core" ecosystem and what does not is quite frankly nonsense. Damage to any part of an ecosystem can potentially shift the boundaries and create a state of disequilibrium, as mentioned earlier.

Chapter 4

ENVIRONMENTAL RAGE

It's not enough to rage against the lie ... you've got to replace it with the truth ...

Bono

The unprecedented rioting that broke out in April 2007 over the Mabira giveaway marked the politicization of the environment. The nexus between environmental and political violence in Africa is not new. Leaders in the environmental movements have often had to face the full might of the state or powerful interest groups.

Most notably, Ken Saro Wiwa, a community leader for the Ogoni people and founder of the Movement for the Survival of the Ogoni People, was hanged with eight others by a Nigerian tribunal on November 10, 1995, after raising the issue of pollution by major oil companies in the Niger Delta.

Others include Dr. Dian Fossey, who dedicated her life to studying and protecting the highland gorilla. She raised the issue internationally of the encroachment of development on the last refuge of the gorillas. In December 1985, she was fighting to prevent thirty-six thousand acres of forestland from being turned into farms; it was also reported that she was about to announce publicly the names of prominent personalities who were behind the poaching and smuggling of endangered species in and out of Rwanda. Before that could happen, she was brutally murdered in her hut on December 27, 1985.

Nobel laureate, the late Dr. Wangari Maathai campaigned against deforestation since the late 1970s, and was arrested several times as she challenged Kenya's environmentally harmful development policies.

Martin Luther King Jr. once said, "When people are caught up in what is right and are willing to suffer for it … nonviolence, effectively organized, is an unstoppable force." The Mabira giveaway led the National Association of Professional Environmentalists (NAPE) to form the Save Mabira Crusade. The government criminalized the peaceful, nonviolent demonstration that the Save Mabira group organized. It then summoned and arrested the leadership, including the chairperson Frank Muramuzi, opposition member of parliament Beatrice Atim Anywar, and Hussein Kyanjo.

Good governance, politics, and environmentalism came to a head on April 12, 2007, in Kampala. During the peaceful demonstration by the Save Mabira Crusade and concerned citizens, the police deployed with disproportional force, which led to rioting and the death of three people. This demonstration marked a watershed moment in Uganda's history; things will no longer be "business as usual." Concerned citizens are not only raising the issue of Mabira but of other government malpractices that may not be in the interest of future generations.

The Mabira outrage, at its core, addressed basic, fundamental human rights. What right does the National Resistance Movement (NRM) government have to deprive the next generation of a biologically diverse ecosystem? The giveaway contravenes the international covenant on economic, social, and cultural rights, of which Article 3 states,

> The state's Parties to the present covenant undertake
> to ensure the equal rights of men and women to the
> enjoyment of all economic, social and cultural rights set
> forth in the present covenant.

A fundamental question ought to be asked: How and why did the environment elicit such an over-the-top response? The police clamped down on the Save Mabira Crusade, and yet in the past, environmentalists were seen as mere irritants. The answer lies in the lack of democratic space, corruption by the political elite, and economic mismanagement.

Al Gore stated that

> Enlightened governments—and their leaders—must play a major role in spreading awareness of the problems in framing practical solutions, in offering a vision of the future we create. But the real work must be done by individuals, and politicians need to assist citizens in their efforts to make new and necessary choices.

He went on to say, "As the dramatic environmental problems in Eastern Europe show, freedom is a necessary condition for an effective stewardship of the environment."[8]

As in Eastern Europe, the agendas of the environmental movement and democracy movements must become conjoined and complementary; the stewardship of the environment and good governance are mutually supportive concepts. The forces and processes working against good governance (not to be confused with good government) work against the stewardship of the environment namely through greed; preoccupation on return on capital as a measure of progress; cronyism, and focus on short-term exploitation at the expense of the long-term equilibrium of a socioeconomic system or ecosystem.

In many countries, greed and a lack of accountability are major causes of environmental destruction. As discussed earlier, environmentalists in Uganda are particularly concerned about who is benefiting from the sale of timber from Mabira. This matter has not been addressed in enough depth to allay suspicion of possible underhanded deals. The Mabira riots ushered in a new age in Ugandan politics; they highlighted the vulnerability of dictatorships that rely on a single strongman and his vision.

---

8   Al Gore, *Earth in the Balance*

If one has only a hammer in one's tool kit, he or she sees all problems as nails to be hammered down. The government's response to the Mabira demonstration is indicative of the NRM's misunderstanding of the significance of the demonstrations and the feelings of the citizenry toward its government. The government's popularity is waning, and the fundamental change the populace expected has not materialized. Meanwhile, the same issues continue, including corruption, failure to resolve ongoing conflict with the Lord's Resistance Army (LRA), militarism abroad (DRC), nepotism, and of course the lack of transparency in the management of Uganda's natural resources—particularly oil.

The environment is only one area in a whole host of grievances Uganda citizens have against the government. The NRM are aware of this and yet treated the demonstrators as the sort of radical environmental group, common in more developed countries, that engages in ecological civil disobedience and ecotage—the sabotaging of equipment to prevent ecological damage in the struggle to preserve wilderness land. Environmentalists in Uganda are not fringe radicals using violent means against property and people; they are everyday folk voicing an emphatic *no* to the politics of exploitation and environmental degradation.

At the core of the Mabira riots lies a fundamental question: Whose development is the president propagating in destroying forests? Forests in Uganda, it is estimated, create about eight hundred fifty thousand jobs in the informal sector. The role of the rural informal sector is ignored in the NRM's pursuit of industrialization using outdated models. Museveni's idea of job creation appears to be limited to a few formal jobs with firms and multinationals closely linked to the ruling elite. The riots were not only about the forest; they were about poverty and elite capture—a cry against the concentration of productive assets in a few hands.

Chapter 5

DEMOCRACY

To have a country one must be a citizen, and share in its sovereignty. Only in a democracy is the State truly the country of all who form it, and can it rely on as many interested defenders of its cause as it numbers citizens.[9]

Maximilien Robespierre,
Discours et rapports a la convention
(Paris: Union Général des Éditions, 1965)

In a modern democracy, parties affected by a political or socioeconomic decision should have their preferences taken into account when the decision is made. Article 7 of the Convention on Access to Information, Public Participation in Decision-Making and Access to Justice in Environmental Matters (Aarhus, Denmark, June 25, 1998) states,

> Each Party shall make appropriate practical and/or other provisions for the public to participate during the preparation of plans and programmes relating to the environment, within a transparent and fair framework, having provided the necessary information to the public.

---

9   Quoted from *Setting the People Free: The Story of Democracy* by John Dunn.

[…] To the extent appropriate, each Party shall endeavour to provide opportunities for public participation in the preparation of policies relating to the environment.

What the above statement presents is an ethical principle stating that affected parties other than decision makers ought to be consulted in a transparent way and with freely accessible information. Winston Churchill, in a speech on November 7, 1909, captured this sentiment perfectly: "Democracy properly understood means the association of all through the leadership of the best."

In regard to the Mabira giveaway, the consent of all stakeholders, the Buganda Kingdom, the Uganda Tourist Board, NFA, and so on was not adequately sought, and the proposal lacked transparency, particularly regarding who will benefit from the sale of timber from the cleared land. What environmentalists had wanted was a participatory consultation process whereby conflicting values of all stakeholders could be evaluated openly and outcomes could be assessed.

In implementing a precautionary principle process, participatory consultation is crucial; it is a way of appealing for prudence and good governance. This requires a change in mind-set and institutional practices, as well as the implementation of new policy measures. It also requires cooperation beyond the simple matter of producing sugar; cooperation needs to be linked with regional and international administrative structures.

The Ugandan environmentalists recognize that protecting Mabira is a value-sensitive issue and that choices made between different courses of action require finding a way to capture the plurality of relevant values and interests. Precaution works best when based on a wide consensus among parliamentarians, NGOs, and social groups who are likely to be affected by the giveaway.

The Mabira demonstrations brought to the fore that the political class (in power and opposition) share a common responsibility for the long-term sustainability of Uganda and that the support for the precautionary principle cannot fully be realized within a framework of power and party politics. The demonstrations also highlight issues of values and decision making. The president pointed out the need for value-added industries as a means of economic emancipation. In response, I quote Paul Hawken:

> If adding value is what business is, or should be, all about, then it follows that you can't contribute values unless you have them. Our personal values, which have become so distant and removed from the juggernauts of commerce, must become increasingly important and finally, integral to the healthy functioning of our economy.[10]

We all make decisions based on subjective value judgments. The Mabira giveaway challenged the value systems and development policy of the NRM government. It highlighted the disconnect of a government used to having its way. Having been in power for over two decades, such a government may now be out of touch with its people.

Past African leaders have not relied on the popular support of the masses to the degree that European leaders have had to during the development of modern states; such African leaders have not been dependent on the type of social contract processes that form the basis of environmental protection and human rights. Rather, they have become experts at consolidating the strength of particular subgroups within their states and using this political power to dominate the body politic. It comes as no surprise, therefore, that the basic conditions for a collective environmental agenda would manifest themselves in demonstrations.

Nevertheless, it is important to point out that organizations such as the National Environment Management Authority (NEMA) have addressed issues of localizing global environmental conventions, such as the Convention

---

10   Quoted from *The Ecology of Commerce* by Paul Hawken.

on Biological Diversity and the Framework Convention on Climate Change. But NEMA has had to operate in a dispensation characterized by greed and short-term exploitation of natural resources. Essentially, NEMA has had to contend with a government preoccupied with remaining in power and concentrating on short-term political concerns. Nevertheless, NEMA has been able to highlight the unsatisfactory implementations of environmental conventions and has suggested possible solutions.

First, NEMA identified weak linkages with development issues. It recognized that environmental protection is seldom effective when a restrictive definition of the environment, like the one espoused by the president in his Mabira giveaway article, is used. A definition that ignores human socioeconomic and cultural activities and systems is void and does not capture the spirit of Agenda 21, in which the environment and human development are complementary and mutually dependent.

Institutional fragmentation within national structures is another factor evidenced by defused responsibilities for environmental conventions among different ministries, with minimal coordination between them. For example, NEMA is responsible for CBD; the Ministry of Agriculture, Animal Industry, and Fisheries for the Convention to Combat Desertification (CCD); the Department of Meteorology in the Ministry of Water, Lands, and Environment for the Framework Convention on Climate Change (UNFCCC); and the Wetlands Inspection Division (also of the Ministry of Water, Lands, and Environment, for the Ramsar Convention). This has led to the proliferation of too many action programs to address the operation of a large number of conventions.

Possible solutions include identifying the complementary aspects of these conventions and then developing synergies, cross-fertilization modalities, and information-sharing mechanisms. NEMA actually highlighted an example of synergies between the Climate Change Convention, Desertification, and Biodiversity Conventions that are relevant to the Mabira giveaway.

For instance, environmental models predict that most continental interiors will receive lower levels of precipitation and experience higher rates of evapotranspiration due to increased temperatures, leading to a drier terrain and possible drought. Uganda is hampered by weak capacity and a lack of resources to adapt and mitigate against negative impacts of climate due to lack of political will and leadership.

Biodiversity and desertification are linked, and proper management of already degraded land can become as important as carbon sinks. Proper land management opens up the possibility of earning valuable foreign exchange by selling the service of carbon sequestration.

NEMA came up with environmental recommendations that integrate global environmental concerns and are applicable to Mabira. They are reproduced below:

- There should be adequate stakeholder identification and analysis aimed at ensuring adequate representation and effective participation in the planning and implementation processes.
- The stakeholder roles and responsibilities, with respect to coordination, planning, and implementation of local, national, and global environmental concerns, should be identified and clearly defined.
- The planning processes should intentionally integrate local, national, and global environmental concerns accompanied by concrete resource commitments.
- There is need for awareness creation on the importance of the global conventions on environment at all levels.
- The capacity of planners, relevant stakeholders, and the communities to understand and address local, national, and global environmental issues needs to be built at all levels.

The Mabira giveaway is cloaked in the guise of development beneficial to the entire economy. The president talks about "changing the society from peasant to middle class, skilled working class society. This means that the majority of the people should shift from agriculture to industries and services."

He goes on to ascertain that newly industrialized countries like Taiwan, South Korea, Malaysia, and Thailand are more prosperous than Uganda because the percentage of their population in agriculture is small: 6%, 6.4%, 14.5%, and 49%, respectively. This is a misleading and simplistic view. One has got to put the president's hypothesis under closer scrutiny.

Environmentalists are not antidevelopment. On the contrary they are in favor of sustainable development and find it disingenuous of the government to vilify them as agents of backwardness while the government portrays itself as progressive. The president espouses a nineteenth-century development model characterized by building factories as a way to industrialization. This ignores the experiences of and lessons learned by other countries. It is important to analyze twenty-first-century development models that are not harmful to the environment as the way forward if indeed the president is concerned about the socioeconomic welfare of Ugandans.

Let us take the case of Singapore. The first prime minister of the country, Lee Kuan Yew, said in his seminal book *From Third World to First World*, "To achieve First World standards in a Third World region, we set out to transform Singapore into a tropical garden city … I concluded that we needed a department dedicated to the care of trees after they had been planted. I established one in the ministry of national development."

He went on to say, "We planted millions of trees, palms, and shrubs. Greening raised the morale of people and gave them pride in their surroundings. We taught them to care for and not vandalize the trees." Environmentalists in Uganda are not against progress but are actually proponents of sustainable development; the newly industrialized countries of Asia (Asian Tigers) have not ignored their cultural and environmental attributes in developing their economic policies—so much so that tourism in these countries is a booming industry, as evidenced by its rapid recovery from the 1998 Asian financial crisis and the severe acute respiratory syndrome (SARS) outbreak of 2003.

The Asia-Pacific region overtook the Americas as the second largest source of international tourism arrivals. A number of factors have been instrumental behind this spectacular growth, one of which is increased support of government. Government support for ecotourism in Uganda has been lackluster.

Ecotourism is a potential foreign-exchange earner that is both environmentally and culturally sustainable. The Mabira forest, with its unique bird life, deserves a greater consideration by government as an area worthy of attracting ecotourists. A cost-benefit analysis between developing Mabira as an ecotourist area and giving away forestland to Mehta would indicate that Uganda as a nation would benefit more from preserving the forest. Preserving the forest would also translate into the protection of national security.

Development is premised on security—not the dominant, narrow approach to security defined by the NRM (which they have failed to live up to by failing or not wanting to crush the insurgency in northern Uganda) but by a broader definition that includes social, economic, and environmental dimensions.

In 1994 the United Nations Development Programme (UNDP) Human Development Report defined human security as entailing seven distinct categories:

1. Economic security (assured and adequate basic incomes)
2. Food security (physical and affordable access to food)
3. Health security
4. Environmental security (access to safe water, clean air, and nondegraded land)
5. Personal security (lack of physical violence)

6. Community security (lack of ethnic violence)
7. Political security (basic human rights and freedoms)

When environmentalists and their supporters took to the streets in April, they had taken on board the human security concept and challenged the narrow concept and failed policy on national security espoused by the NRM. The demonstrations brought prominence to the issue of security as one involving individuals and communities as demonstrators argued with their feet that environmental integrity is crucial for ensuring security for current and future generations of Ugandans.

The demonstration to preserve Mabira also embraced the spirit of the 1987 Report of the World Commission on Environment and Development (commonly referred to as the Brundtland report after its chairperson), which defined sustainable development as "development that meets the needs of the present without compromising the ability of future generations to meet their own needs." The report identified the critical objectives of sustainable development:

- reviving growth but changing its quality;
- meeting essential needs for employment, food, energy, water and sanitation;
- ensuring a sustainable level of populations;
- conserving and enhancing the resource base;
- reorienting technology and managing risk; and
- merging environment and economics in decision making

This concept overlaps with the human security one and is now receiving increasing content by civil society in discussing national and regional development, national security, law, and democracy. As mentioned earlier, sustainable development ought to be grounded in the fact that natural resources, such as forests, are a form of capital that is not infinite, and the resources' increasing scarcity is a limiting factor in development.

In law, references to sustainable development (and, by extension, to human security) appear in nonbinding texts and national and international judicial pronouncements. The right to development is enshrined in the Rio Declaration, and it stresses that the developmental and environmental needs of present and future generations must be fulfilled equitably (Principle 3).

Principle 4 of the Rio Declaration goes on to merge environmental and development concerns by pointing out that in order to achieve sustainable development, environmental protection shall constitute an integral part of the development process; the two are complementary and have to be considered together.

Chapter 6

SUSTAINABLE DEVELOPMENT

We owe it to ourselves and to posterity to demonstrate that modern development is possible without sacrifice in equality and humanity which has everywhere accompanied "development" of the present industrialized states.

Julius Kambarage Nyerere

In September 2000, representatives from 189 nations, including Uganda, endorsed the United Nations Millennium Declaration[11] and resolved to commit themselves to making development a right for the entire human race. The declaration called for the halving, by the year 2015, of the number of people who live on less than one dollar a day. This initiative also involves supporting the Agenda 21 principles of sustainable development.

The United Nations secretariat and the specialized agencies of the UN system, as well as representatives of IMF, the World Bank, and OECD, defined a set of targets for combating poverty and environmental degradation, among other goals. The political framework for achieving the Millennium Development Goals are outlined in an agreement between north and south agreed upon in Monterrey, Mexico, in 2002.

---

11   United Nations Millennium Declaration, RES/55/2.

Without dwelling too much on the details of the Millennium Development Goals, it is important to point out that the Mabira giveaway is contrary to the spirit of the Millennium Declaration in that it links environmental degradation with industrialization through multinational corporations such as the Mehta Group. The president ignores totally the importance of small and medium enterprises (SMEs) to sustainable development. SMEs provide 90 percent of Uganda's off-farm employment and over 20 percent of total employment, providing a vital link with multinationals and producing 20 percent of Uganda's GDP.

A considerable amount of work has been done on the role and importance of SMEs to the development process, and it is apparent that it is through the promotion of SMEs that countries like Uganda can make progress toward reaching the global target of halving poverty by the year 2015. The Uganda government has been integrating itself into the global economy through economic liberalism in ways that favor a select few without promoting and empowering SMEs effectively.

The need to industrialize at the expense of the environment is not a new position, and the Mabira giveaway is not the first of its kind. In 2002 the government degazetted Butamira Forest Reserve, displacing tree farmers so that Kakira Sugar Works could grow sugarcane. The Namanve Forest Reserve is another example whereby 1,006 hectares of forestland was gazetted for an industrial park. The president is quite proud of this industrial park, mentioning that the Coca-Cola factory is there employing seven hundred people. He goes on to extrapolate that one thousand factories could employ seven hundred thousand persons.

It is precisely this kind of example that irks some progressives in Uganda. Of all the progressive Uganda companies, the president chose to mention the Coca-Cola factory. The message is clear: "Let us all drink Coke and industrialize!" But on a serious note, Coca-Cola capitalism will not get Ugandans very far on the road to development. First, Uganda's ruling political elite have tended to have links with multinationals like Coca-Cola and have enriched themselves at the exclusion of SMEs and peasants who constitute the core of the private sector. One has to look into who has a stake in the Coca-Cola factory in Uganda to realize that personal aspirations of elites are being dressed up as development.

Furthermore, the Coca-Cola Company is not a good example of a company that champions social responsibility and development, given the recent accusations by communities in India that the company is draining precious water resources, as well as polluting the land and water. These complaints led to one of Coca-Cola's largest bottling plants in India to shut down in March 2004. To deflect this negative criticism in India, the company joined the United Nations Global Compact.

The United Nations Global Compact is a framework for businesses that are committed to aligning their operations and strategies with ten universally accepted principles in the areas of human rights, labor, the environment, and anticorruption. The response of holding the company responsible has resulted in the Coca-Cola Company being dropped from the socially responsible investment fund of TIAA-CREF, the largest pension fund in the world.

Ugandans in general do not have a quarrel with Coca-Cola per se, but when the president mentions a company by name, one needs to scrutinize the company. Past history of linkages between companies and ruling elites demands this.

The irony of mentioning Coca-Cola is that the company has stopped using sugar as a sweetener for its US products, preferring to use high-fructose corn syrup (HFCS). Although it must be said that Coca-Cola uses sugar in other nations. HFCS is primarily used in the production of HFCS 55, which in terms of sweetness is comparable to table sugar (sucrose); HFCS 90 is sweeter than sucrose. Sugar producers around the world are monitoring this trend of using HFCS as an alternative to sugar among multinational corporations.

Technology, trade, and economics have come together to make HFCS a preference over sugar, largely due to US import quotas and tariffs on sugar. These tariffs significantly increase the domestic US price for sugar. The only reason I mention this here is that the United States, where the Coca-Cola parent company is located, has not been particularly friendly to sugar producers from the developing world. I am not blaming the United States; rather, I am pointing out that technological innovations and trade regimes can derail a country's development strategy if they are not well thought through. The destruction of Mabira is a case in point.

It is quite understandable that the United States and Canada prefer HFCS, for it is somewhat cheaper, due to the abundance of corn; it is easier to blend and transport; and it leads to products with a much longer shelf life. In regard to the sugar industry, Uganda should abandon nineteenth-century models of development and look at exploiting its natural and comparative economic advantage in the global market.

The widespread use of HFCS in Canada and the United States only goes to show that the economic and scientific landscape has changed considerably. Green issues (like saving Mabira) today are not fringe matters but are mainstream and deserve greater consideration by government. Preserving our forests opens up opportunities through the development of new innovative markets such as carbon sequestration, biodiversity conservation, and ecotourism.

Ecotourism also not need be an arrangement between elites and MNEs; it can involve local communities directly. A good example of this is the Uganda Community Tourism Association (UCOTA), which was established in July 1998 to empower local communities in sustainable development through small-scale tourism, also known as community tourism.

Community tourism aims at involving the local people in the planning, decision making, and implementing of tourism-development activities. This form of tourism has the attribute of concentrating benefits at the local community level. By 2006 UCOTA had fifty member groups countrywide, representing about 1,200 individuals, of whom 63 percent are women.

On June 5, 2008, at the opening of the third session of the eighth Parliament, President Museveni reiterated that the Mabira giveaway was still in the cards. He said, "Mehta (part owners of the Sugar Corporation of Uganda Limited) wanted some land to increase sugar production and employment, some confused groups tried to frustrate these programs (but) with patience these will be solved."

It is clear that the debate on Mabira is still an emotive issue that is yet to be resolved, and the "enemies of progress" or "confused groups," as the president is wont to call environmentalists, face an uphill battle in convincing the government to reconsider the giveaway.

This divergence of opinion about sustainable development, which is the essence of the conflict between the government and environmentalist, is not new. It entered the political discourse some time ago; after ten years of study, the International Law Association Committee on Legal Aspects of Sustainable Development released the 2002 New Delhi Declaration on the Principles of International Law Related to Sustainable Development.[12]

Without claiming to be exhaustive, the New Delhi Declaration identified seven principles:

1. The duty of states to ensure sustainable use of natural resources
2. The principle of equity and eradication of poverty
3. The principle of common but differentiated responsibility
4. The principle of the precautionary approach to human health, natural resources, and ecosystems
5. The principle of public participation and access to information and justice

---

12   ILA Resolution 3/2002: New Delhi Declaration of Principles of International Law Relating to Sustainable Development, in ILA, Report of the Seventieth Conference, New Delhi (London: ILA, 2002). Available online at http://www.ila-hq.org.

6. The principle of good governance
7. The principle of integration and interrelationship, in particular in relation to human rights and social, economic, and environmental objectives

The Mabira giveaway, I contend, violates most, if not all, of these principles. I shall go through each principle in turn to highlight this point, starting with Principle 1. During the 2002 World Summit on Sustainable Development, "protecting and managing the natural resource base of economic and social development" was a paramount tenet. The 1992 Rio Declaration, in Principle 2, affirms the responsibility to avoid causing harm to the environment of other states, although Uganda has the sovereign right to exploit its natural resources.

However, the Mabira forest is part of a wider ecosystem encompassing the Lake Victoria basin. At the time of writing, the greater East African region is facing drought, and this crisis is further being compounded by armed conflict in parts of the region, most notably in Somalia. It is in this regard that the Mabira giveaway violates Principle 1 of the New Delhi Declaration, in that although the Mabira forest is in Uganda and therefore a domestic resource, the harm of misusing this resource has transboundary implications.

The main problem here is scientifically articulating that converting parts of Mabira into a sugarcane plantation constitutes unsustainable use and that this use has negative impacts beyond the Uganda borders. Although the science may be weak in supporting this view, such a lack of data is precisely why a precautionary approach should be adopted, particularly because the precautionary approach applies when

- there exist scenarios of possible environmental harm that are based on some scientifically plausible reasoning;
- the potential environmental harm is sufficiently serious for present and/or future generations to find unacceptable;

- time is of the essence and that there is a need to act promptly, since effective counteraction later will be considerably more difficult and costly; and

- there exist scientific uncertainties.

It is therefore imperative that a participatory, sustainable management approach is adopted for Mabira whereby long-term natural-resource planning and management systems are put in place that can predict or at least estimate sustained yield or thresholds for resource collapse. On visiting the Mehta Group website, the only statement one sees on sustainable use of resources is "we shall manage land and wetlands resources in an environmentally sensitive manner, and employ energy efficient technologies and procedures."

It is clear that the Mehta Group's environmental policy is geared toward operational issues, which is fine, but environmentalists are not interested in a situation whereby a factory is using environmentally sensitive procedures to destroy an ecosystem. It is like feeding someone slow-acting poison and congratulating yourself that you are providing three square meals a day, regardless of the fact the food is laced with poison and that one is, in effect, killing by feeding.

In regard to the second principle and the eradication of poverty, it is important to first reflect on the definition of "sustainable development" provided by the World Commission on Environment and Development in their *Our Common Future* report, which states that the "overriding priority" should be given to the "concept of needs, particularly the essential needs of the world's poor. This remains an essential pillar of sustainable development."[13]

Many of the international instruments on environment and development are influenced by the *Our Common Future* report. Indeed, Chapter II of the Johannesburg Plan of Implementation focuses on the eradication of poverty

13   World Commission on Environment and Development, *Our Common Future* (Oxford: University Press, 1987).

for sustainable development. Such concepts were strongly reinforced and highlighted in the 2002 World Summit on Sustainable Development.[14]

The Johannesburg Plan of Implementation strategies for poverty eradication cannot be overemphasized. Concrete measures are required to enable developing countries such as Uganda to achieve sustainable development goals; these goals include those contained in Agenda 21 and the United Nations Millennium Declaration. These would prompt actors at all levels to "combat desertification and mitigate the effects of drought and floods through measures such as improved use of ... land and natural resources management, agricultural practices and ecosystem conservation in order to reverse current trends and minimize degradation of land and water resources ..."

The Mabira giveaway does not address poverty eradication comprehensively, although the president tries unsuccessfully to link the destruction of part of the forest to higher employment and more tax revenues for government to fight poverty. This is a flawed premise, because the number of Ugandans and East Africans who rely on a stable Great Lakes, Horn of Africa ecosystem far exceeds the number who will benefit directly from the Mabira giveaway.

Negative environmental impacts (drought) are already evident in the region; the falling water level of Lake Victoria is affecting the fishing industry and approximately seven hundred thousand people. Some experts believe this is partly due to poorly designed hydroelectric projects that may have not carried out a comprehensive Environmental Impact Assessment (EIA).

This leads to Principle 6—namely, good governance. Good governance obliges states and international organizations to uphold the tenets of democratic and transparent decision making; anticorruption; and respect

---

14   In the Johannesburg Declaration on Sustainable Development, states committed themselves to "building a humane, equitable and caring global society, cognizant of the need for human dignity for all."

for the rule of law and human rights. It is also linked to the principle of participation and access to information and justice.

Good governance is essential for sustainable development. In the giveaway article, the president mentions Taiwan, South Korea, and Malaysia and how they have achieved the status of newly industrialized countries by moving away from agriculture. What he does not mention is that these countries also had to fight corruption and institute a culture and practice of good governance at all levels of government.

Without a policy to create clean government and curb corruption, Uganda will not industrialize. At the moment, this is a serious concern of many Ugandans; hence the outrage about the giveaway. In the eyes of many, the government is not perceived as clean. This is evident when one sees the Transparency International's Corruption Perception Index (CPI),[15] in which, out of 179 countries, Uganda ranked 111th. The countries mentioned by the president, Taiwan, South Korea, and Malaysia, ranked 34th, 43rd, and 43rd, respectively.

Quite frankly, given the government's record on natural-resources exploitation, the Mabira giveaway does not engender confidence that this is being done in the interest of the greater good and for the benefit of Uganda as a whole. So the corollary that giving forestland to manufacturers will lead to more government tax revenues is only true where there is good governance. In a study for the Cato Institute, Andrew Mwenda, a prominent Ugandan journalist and at one time the political editor of the *Monitor*, highlighted a number of issues regarding Uganda's taxation policy that point to at least weak, if not bad, government.

Mwenda noted that tax collection by Uganda Revenue Authority amounts to around 12 percent of GDP, which he points out is below the sub-Saharan African average of 18–20 percent and below the government's target of 24

---

15   http:// www.transparency.org/policy_research/surveys_indices/cpi/2007 (assessed Oct 15, 2007)

percent. Also, the rich and politically connected don't pay taxes. In other words, the giveaway is unlikely to alleviate poverty in Uganda.

The 1987 Report of the World Commission on Environment and Development addresses the issue of future generations as follows:

> Many present efforts to guard and maintain human progress, to meet human needs, and to realize human ambitions are simply unsustainable in both the rich and poor nations. They draw too heavily, too quickly; on already overdrawn environmental resource accounts to be affordable far into the future without bankrupting those accounts ... We act as we do because we can get away with it: future generations do not vote, they have no political or financial power; they cannot challenge our decisions. But the results of the present profligacy are rapidly closing the options for future generations.

Uganda's quest to industrialize has got to be juxtaposed with experiences of other nations that have achieved massive growth over the last forty years. Ireland, for example, in the 1960s was one of the poorest countries in Western Europe; from 1987 it had one of the fastest growing economies in the European Union. It did this through innovative state-transformation strategies, including an intergenerational approach that takes care of the elderly people and people with disabilities while investing in the future for its youth. It did this by implementing social and economic programmes via social partnerships between the state and economic and social interests.

The example of Ireland brings up the issue of intragenerational equity. Intragenerational equity is directed at the serious socioeconomic asymmetry in resource access and use within and between societies and nations that has exacerbated environmental degradation. In Uganda the intragenerational gap is wide; the divide between rich and poor is considerable, and the insurgency in northern Uganda has left millions to exist on humanitarian handouts in IDP camps. To environmentalists, the Mabira giveaway only widens the intragenerational gap. It excludes and punishes many and will only benefit a few in the short run before it becomes unsustainable.

The principle of common and differentiated responsibility recognizes the historical differences of developing and developed countries, and this is reflected in the UN Framework Convention on Climate Change that states in Article 3(1) that

> The Parties should protect the climate system for the benefit of present and future generations of humankind, on the basis of equity and in accordance with their common but differentiated responsibilities and respective capabilities. Accordingly, the developed country Parties should take the lead in combating climate change and the adverse effects thereof.

In adhering to the principle of differentiated responsibilities by developing countries like Uganda, an important financial mechanism needs to be in place, such as the Global Environment Facility (GEF),[16] which supports activities of developing countries to comply with the UN Framework Convention on Climate Change, the UN Convention on Biological Diversity, and the UN Convention to Combat Desertification.

This mechanism provides financial grants for implementing sustainable development projects. Could this mechanism be used to mitigate the possible effects of the giveaway or urge government to undertake a more community-oriented approach to the giveaway? I don't know, but this ought to be looked into. The influence of donors cannot be ignored. Dr. Nyangabyaki Bazaara of the Center for Basic Research stated,

> Environmental issues appear to have entered the policy and legislative realm mainly as a result of pressures

---

16   The GEF provides resources in the areas of climate change, biodiversity, pollution of international water courses, and depletion of the ozone layer. In 2002, desertification was added as a focus for GEF funding.

from donors, who made the implementation of certain environmental-related programs a condition for the Uganda government to access grants or loans. Such was the case with the European Economic Community, which insisted that all encroaches in forest and game reserves be evicted before it could release funds to the Uganda government.[17]

It is important to point out that the issue of financial grants also leads back to the principle of good governance mentioned earlier. The world's largest AIDS fund has been victim of a multimillion-pound fraud. The Fraud Office has been sent a file on alleged corruption involving a program run by the Global Fund to Fight AIDS, TB, and Malaria, worth 4.2 billion GBP.[18] A number of prominent Ugandans close to the seat of power have been implicated in this fraud, and many Ugandans are not satisfied in the way it is being addressed by government. Donor funds are welcome, but stringent oversight and accountability protocols have to be improved upon.

The principle of precaution has already been addressed, and therefore I will only reiterate that Article 15 of the 1992 Rio Declaration on Environment and Development states,

> In order to protect the environment, the precautionary approach shall be widely applied by States according to their capabilities. Where there are threats of serious or irreversible damage, lack of scientific certainty shall not be used as a reason for postponing cost-effective measures to prevent environmental degradation.

In other words, precaution regarding human health, natural resources, and ecosystems means, within the Mabira giveaway context, that if the giveaway might lead to either significant, serious, or irreversible harm, the

---

17   Dr. Nyangabyaki Bazaara, "Decentralization Politics and Environment in Uganda," World Resources Institute, 2003.
18   *Times* online, September 16, 2007.

government is obligated to take measures (or permit measures to be taken) to prevent this damage (including halting the proposed activity), even if there is lack of full scientific certainty as to the existence and severity of the risk.

The degree of harm needed to trigger the principle depends on the provisions of the relevant soft law:

(1)   Rio Declaration Principle 15, 1992, and

(2)   World Summit on Sustainable Development (WSSD) Johannesburg Declaration, 2002.

The principle also depends on the stipulations of treaty law—for example, in the Biodiversity Convention, it is when there is a "threat of significant reduction or loss of biological diversity"; in the Bamako Convention, it is when an activity "may cause harm to humans or the environment."

Precaution is recommended regarding the Mabira forest because there are high risks of "possible harm," and even when the lower risks of "serious and irreversible harm" apply, this remains the case. Precaution is balanced by proportionality: The magnitude of the risk to the Mabira forest is considered in tandem with whether the magnitude of damage, should harm occur, would be high or low.

Moving forward with the Mabira giveaway does not conform to the principle of public participation and access to information and justice. Public participation is closely linked to human rights. Alexander Kiss, Director of Research Emeritus at the Centre National de la Recherche Scientifique, France, and professor at the Robert Schuman University of Strasbourg, and Dinah Shelton, professor of international law at George Washington University, who has served as legal consultant to the United Nations Environment Programme, World Health Organization, European Union, and the Council of Europe and Organization of American States, state, "Public participation is based on the right of those who may be affected to have a say in the determination of their environmental future."[19] Given the importance of forests to the entire Great Lakes region, those affected add up to a significantly large number of people.

The April demonstrations can therefore be seen as a public expression of anger about the trampling of the right to participate. The UN Committee on Economic, Social, and Cultural Rights has indicated that this principle is essential to the realization of economic, social, and cultural rights. It states that rights of individuals and groups to participate in decision-making processes that may affect development must be an integral component of any policy developed to implement government obligations under the right to health. Incidentally, the Baganda and other tribes use the forest to harvest medicine during pregnancy and childbirth.

The 1981 African Charter on Human and Peoples' Rights was the first international human-rights instrument to contain an explicit guarantee of environmental quality. Article 24 specifically states that "All peoples shall have the right to a general satisfactory environment favorable to their development." It should also be stated that the National Forestry and Tree Planting Act (2003) encourages "public participation in the management and conservation of forests and trees." But when the public demonstrated in April, was it a sign of a disconnect between the public and government?

Dr. Nyangabyaki Bazaara identified in 2003 that "the unstable nature of forestry legislation has also contributed to a series of crises within the Forestry Department that have in turn made it difficult for local governments to apply the environmental powers given to them by law."

The last Principle of Integration and Interrelationship in Relation to Social Economic and Environmental Objectives correlates with Principle 4 of the 1992 Rio Declaration, which states, "in order to achieve sustainable

---

19   Alexander Kiss, and Dinah Shelton, *International Environmental Law*, 2nd ed. (New York: Transnational Publishers, 1994).

development, environmental protection shall constitute an integral part of the development process and cannot be considered in isolation from it."

Environmentalists believe that environmental objectives have been overlooked in Uganda's quest to industrialize at all costs. The divergent views between the president and environmentalists continue, as no common-ground solutions have been adequately pursued.

A report prepared by the Multi-Stakeholder Integrative Sustainability Planning Project (MISP) Task Force, "Localizing Global Environmental Conventions: Opportunities for Integrating Four Selected Conventions in Planning Processes on Uganda," for the National Environment Management Authority through funding by GEF mechanism, stated: "environmental protection is seldom effective when a restrictive definition of the environment is used, that does not include human activities and systems." This captures the essence of the conflict between the president and the environmentalists; the giveaway does not address issues of "human activity and (eco) systems sufficiently."

Chapter 7

TOWARD A KNOWLEDGE-BASED ECONOMY

Wealth does not arise from fields, factories, offices and machines. And revolutionary wealth is not just about money ... The importance of knowledge in wealth creation has steadily grown and is now about to leap to a much higher level and cross additional borders as more parts of the world play in to ever growing, ever changing, ever more accessible planetary brain bank.

Alvin and Heidi Toffler,
Revolutionary Wealth

Basing twenty-first-century industrialization efforts on nineteenth-century models is absurd. Destroying Uganda's forests (of which the true value is unknown) to pursue industrialization models of past centuries can only be described as dysfunctional development. Alvin and Heidi Toffler, in their seminal bestseller *Revolutionary Wealth*, pointed out that "No wealth system can sustain itself without a host society and culture. And the host and culture themselves are shaken up as two or more wealth systems collide." The wealth systems the Tofflers are talking about manifest themselves in three waves. The first wave is based on growing things, and the second on making things. The third-wave wealth system is increasingly based on serving, thinking, knowing, and experiencing. Each wealth system can be symbolized by the plow, the assembly line, and the computer.

The Mabira giveaway advocates an industrial model that ignores and is out of step with the realities of the twenty-first-century knowledge-based economy. The newly industrialized countries around the world have established development programs that tap into the knowledge-based economy.

Visionary leaders like Jawaharal Nehru, India's first prime minister, were ahead of the curve. Nehru was often criticized for investing heavily in Indian technological institutes. India's growing economy from financial services to information technology today is a result of Nehru's investment in human capital. The impact of the information revolution on trade, markets, and development in general cannot be overstated. This revolution questions our assumptions about information, knowledge, and wisdom.

The giveaway ignores the probable impact of a knowledge-based economy on the sugar industry and market in East Africa and in the Common Market of Eastern and Southern Africa (COMESA) region. Uganda's Poverty Eradication Action Plan (PEAP 2004/5–2007/8) and draft documents of the National Development Plan (NDP) highlight the importance of science and technology for economic transformation while noting that Uganda's current science and technology capacity is not in sync with President Museveni's aspirations of industrialization.

Government's record in bolstering a knowledge-based economy leaves a lot to be desired. Government focus has in recent years been in the information and communications technologies (ICT), but not with the zeal and passion of Rwanda, which is aiming to be the regional ICT hub. Technological buffs in Uganda feel that Uganda should be the ICT hub for the region, given its unique geographical position and ability to attract investment and provide quality services through dedicated manpower.

How does the president expect Uganda to industrialize when studies show that basic science enrollment is only 0.6 percent of overall tertiary enrollment (perhaps about 450 students for the whole country)? The number of students studying for "science and engineering" degrees is likely to be no more than 2–3 percent of total tertiary enrollment. A country cannot industrialize with a poor "culture of science." A World Bank report states that fewer than 550 professors in Uganda have PhDs, and fewer than eight new PhDs are awarded annually in the sciences and engineering disciplines nationally.

Are the Ugandan people being taken for a ride about industrialization when in fact what is happening is the elite capture and destruction of a national asset? The lies about Uganda's great strides as a progressive democratic and modern economy know no bounds. For instance, at the Kololo Airstrip on October 25, 2010, President Museveni, after his nomination as flag bearer for NRM, said that if he was re-elected as president, he would send a Ugandan into outer space and even to the moon as part of Uganda's prolific scientific achievements. This kind of nonsense is insulting to most Ugandans even during a run-up to an election.

Let us not forget that we will not industrialize overnight and that agriculture, forestry, and fisheries contribute about a third of Uganda's GDP, worth an estimated US$2 billion according to official statistics. And yet most universities in Uganda do not conduct research in these sectors or disciplines, with the exception of Makerere and Mbarara Universities and a few emerging high-quality private institutions. Contrast this with Britain, which has eight universities in the world's top fifty. British researchers get the highest number of citations and publish more papers per researcher than in France, Germany, Italy, Japan, the United States, Canada, and Russia.[20] The path to development and industrialization is through the application of innovative ways of exploiting our forests and other natural resources. Such an application will be based on science; technology; financial and economical instruments; and an enabling environment that is able to exploit natural resources in innovative ways for the twenty-first century. Plantation farming is a nineteenth-century development model inappropriate for the Uganda of the future.

---

20   Jonathan Grant and Joachim Krupels, "Science and Technology Policy," in Varum Uberoi, Adam Coutts, Iain Mclean, and David Halpern, eds., *Options for a New Britain* (Palgrave Macmillan, 2009).

To industrialize, the state has to develop a supportive infrastructure for industry. For example, the United Kingdom under Tony Blair's New Labour reestablished its science base with a 63 percent surge in science expenditure. A national innovation system—the Technology Strategy Board, Technology Foresight, and the billion-pound Innovation Fund—was established to help Britain become competitive in a knowledge economy. The NRM government has done little in setting up supportive architecture for industrialization, and Ugandans are not convinced that current policy will lead to any meaningful development.

In a knowledge-based economy, the role of technology will be critical in development programming; simply destroying biodiversity to introduce monocultural agriculture is not enough to be competitive in the twenty-first century. The sugar industry itself is undergoing significant changes; the increasing use of HFCS is a case in point. In the COMESA region, changes are also taking place. For example, COMESA wants sugar millers to adopt a new pricing formula that would pay farmers based on sucrose content rather than on cane tonnage.

On the other hand, the president states that for Mehta to be competitive, the company would have to increase production from "present level of 55,000 tonnes per annum to 110,000 tonnes per annum. In order to do that he needs 1.2 million tones of sugar cane per annum, which can only be produced on 22,500 hectares of usable land … he needs an extra 7,100 hectares from government." Extra tonnage may not mean much if variety of sugarcane planted has low sucrose content. The role of technology in producing early-maturing, high-sucrose varieties highlights technology as an area to invest in. When COMESA pricing goes into effect, it may well be that Uganda will have destroyed a valuable ecosystem for very little economic benefit.

Kenya is already investing in knowledge for economic progress, as it is already researching high-sucrose and early-maturing cane varieties with the Kenya Sugar Board (KSB) and Kenya Sugar Research Foundation (KSREF).

Environmentalists, economists, development planners, and concerned citizens are asking themselves whether Uganda can honestly compete in sugar production against other regional countries, namely Sudan, Kenya, and Tanzania. In a global economy, one should be thinking in broad terms and in terms of the East African market, which is around one hundred million people. Destroying Mabira to cater only to the Ugandan market only shows that the NRM government is behind the curve on understanding the opportunities available in gearing corporate Uganda to exploit this market.

A knowledge-based economy essentially is rooted in globalization; countries that ignore this will be left behind. In traveling around East Africa, it is clear that Ugandan labor, both skilled and unskilled, and capital have crossed our borders to exploit economic opportunities regionally and abroad. Ugandans abroad send remittances back home to the tune of US$600 million a year.

A "failed state" like Somalia is able to survive in a global economy because the Somalis in the diaspora remit funds to relatives back home at lower cost and more quickly than most other transfer services worldwide. Somalia also has one of the cheapest mobile telephone networks in East Africa. Entrepreneurship is alive in Somalia, and it just goes to show that governments do not have the monopoly of knowledge or sound economic policy.

Destroying Mabira and other forests in the DRC and Kenya will impact the regional climate without a doubt. The effects of forest destruction are severe and irreversible, while the benefits of a small increase in sugar production as compared to the potential market are minimal.

It is fundamental to an understanding of sustainable development that the economy is not separate from the environment. Knowledge of this is crucial in development planning and in agro-industrialization. We have to take particular care in establishing that environmental losses in monocultural agriculture can be significant; even if the environmental damage is insignificant, it pays for us to leave Mabira intact and re-evaluate, because social and economic costs incurred later on are preferable to costs incurred now.

The two issues here are

- the value of the Mabira ecosystem, and
- the costs and benefit of anticipatory policy.

In valuing the Mabira ecosystem, the central problem is that many of the services provided by the Mabira forest are deemed to be free. In other words, the Mabira forest has a zero-price supply because no formal marketplace exists in which its true value can be revealed through the acts of buying and selling.

The important principle here is to recognize that resources and environments serve economic functions and have positive economic value. The economic theory of supply and demand tells us that if something is provided at a zero price, more of it will be demanded than if there were a positive price. In other words, the cheaper it is, the more will be demanded. The looting of the DRC's timber by Ugandan military officers and their proxies highlights this economic theory; to the looters, the timber in the DRC is free. They got away with it (at least for now) and are trying to do the same with the Mabira forest.

Greed and personal profit are what fuelled the looting of the DRC. It is important to note that the Congo's rain forests are the world's second largest after the Amazon, and expected deforestation up to the year 2050 is set to release over thirty-four billion tons of carbon dioxide gas.[21] It is important to point out here that Uganda is not the only or even the major culprit in forest destruction in the DRC. Nevertheless, as environmentalists like to say, "think global, act local." We should do our part locally in fighting deforestation whenever we can, and the first step is to acknowledge that the

21   www.greenpeace.org/raw/content/international/press/reports/carving-up-the-congo-exec.pdf

Mabira forest has a positive value. We can then determine this value and integrate this value into a knowledge-based economic and development policy.

Moving on to the cost and benefit of our anticipatory and reactive environmental policy: The potential of irreversibly destroying our forests is real. We therefore cannot continue with business as usual and rely on reactive policy when environmental damage is happening. Reactive environmental strategies should be undertaken only if they can be "afforded" by the future; of course, what the future can afford depends on what we lease them by way of inherited wealth, natural and man-made. In President Museveni's giveaway, he tends to propose a reactive, rather than a robust, anticipatory environmental policy.

Proper Pricing of Mabira

It has often been said that knowledge is power, and knowledge of the value of the Mabira forest and other natural resources is the basis of formulating a sound, environmentally friendly development program for Uganda. One way of pricing the Mabira is by using a marginal social cost pricing.

Marginal social cost pricing is often used in valuing natural-resource use. This model espouses that any natural resource should be priced so that the price reflects the (marginal) cost of extraction or harvesting and the marginal external cost (MEC) of any damage done by using the resource. For an exhaustible resource, however, there is an additional component to price. This is so because extracting and using a unit of a natural exhaustible resource today means that it is not available for use in the future. Basically, current use precludes future use. The associated cost is termed "user cost." We could then write the formula for the "proper" pricing of a natural resource, such as a forest, as

$$P = MC + MEC + MUC = MOC$$

Whereby

P = Price

MC = Marginal Cost

MEC = Marginal External Cost

MUC = Marginal User Cost

MOC = Marginal Opportunity Cost

One should note that if resource extraction does not incur external costs and if there are reasons to believe MUC is very small, the pricing rule would be approximately achieved by a competitive market.

It can also be argued that MUC will be reflected in current prices; however, that will depend on how accurately current markets reflect future scarcity, an issue that is constantly being debated among economists. Nevertheless, for many natural resources, including the Mabira forest, future impact will be considerable (e.g., as a result of climatic change impacts due to deforestation).

In conclusion, the economic principles underlying the "proper" pricing of goods and services and of natural resources are the same in that prices should reflect the true social costs of production and use. Essentially, this means reflecting the true socioeconomic and cultural values of environmental products in prices, rather than treating natural resources as free goods. In the president's giveaway article, he comes across as regarding Mabira as a free good; not once is any value attributed to the forest as a whole, or, surprisingly, to the "free" timber that will be harvested for sugar. The question: Is this an oversight or a deliberate move so that some fat cats can again exploit this national resource for personal gain? We might never know.

A knowledge-based economy should be based on value, technology, intellectual property rights, and markets. There is an adage that says a cynic is someone who knows the price of everything and the value of nothing. The government does not see the value of the Mabira forest and can only price it in terms of timber to be sold or sugar produced.

In neighboring Tanzania, there is growing awareness and knowledge of the economic value of forests as a source of income for rural people through the production of honey (a healthier alternative than processed sugar as a sweetener) and beeswax. Sales are measured at around US$2 million a year with the potential of going up to US$100 million a year.[22] The importance of bees in pollination, food crops, and plants in general is largely forgotten by many; nevertheless, the Tanzanians are following a more ecofriendly exploitation of their forests based on an understanding of the true value of its forest resources.

A knowledge-based economy should be capable of developing products and instruments, based on the underlying value of the Mabira forest, that can benefit Ugandan citizens as a whole. Experts believe that the next financial revolution will be in the convergence of financial markets and the environment. The use of derivatives (a financial instrument whose value is based on another security) based on the value of Uganda's natural resources to be traded internationally should be explored.

Former United States vice president Al Gore, in his 2007 book *The Assault on Reason*, highlighted the importance of "knowledge as a source of influence" and its impact on politics and economics in the United States. He points out,

… the information revolution in the last quarter of the twentieth century transformed economic output by substituting ingenuity for raw materials (the total value of everything produced in the American economy grew by 300 percent from 1950 to 2000, while the gross tonnage remained the same) …

---

22   Based on average prices in 2003 of US$1 per kilogram of honey and US$2 per kilogram of beeswax.

As already mentioned earlier, Kenya is applying knowledge to the sugar industry, while Uganda is still thinking in terms of increasing gross tonnage. The way forward for Uganda is through the application of technology and knowledge to add value to what we already produce without further destroying our environment.

The problem is governments like the NRM are wont to argue that because Europe and North America fueled their nineteenth-century industrial development with deforestation and other forms of environmental degradation, developing countries like Uganda should not be subjected to a different standard. Second, they argue that if preserving the rain forests benefits the wealthier, developed countries, the poorer developing countries should not bear the cost of preservation. Furthermore, preservation does not benefit the NRM cronies. Preserving Mabira may make the world a better place but does not make the corrupt leaders better off, and the president is convinced that Uganda will be worse off economically.

How can the environmentalists convince President Museveni to change his thinking about Mabira? First, we should advise him that in a modern knowledge-based economy, the value of a forest like Mabira has more value as a living forest rather than as lumber or as a sugarcane field.

Environmentalists are also bemused at the NRM government's contradictory policies toward the environment. On the one hand, environmentalists are vilified as lunatics, but then the government undertakes, through the NFA, the Nile Basin Reforestation project in exchange for revenues from the World Bank BioCarbon Fund. Meanwhile, the very logic of preserving Mabira is questioned and deemed to be antidevelopment. Should Uganda destroy its forests (and biodiversity) only to undertake reforestation projects? This is why many Ugandans feel that one of the primary reasons for the giveaway is for politically connected elite to benefit from the timber. Mabira must be preserved and used productively.

Debt for Nature Swaps

One way forward is the use of Mabira in a debt-for-nature swap. The idea of debt-for-nature swaps was first proposed by Dr. Thomas Lovejoy, chief biodiversity adviser to the president of the World Bank. A debt-for-nature swap is an agreement between an organization (usually NGO) and a forested country like Uganda. It would work like this: A NGO buys and retires a portion of Uganda's external debt in exchange for a promise to preserve the Mabira forest.

Uganda's external debt (US $1.498 billion on December 31, 2007) is a tremendous drain on the economy. The Bank of Uganda annual report for 2008 to Parliament stated that the total foreign debt stock increased from US $1.47 billion last financial year to US $1.99 billion. Since the banks holding the debt view their prospects for full and timely repayment as problematic, the debt can be purchased by the NGO for a fraction of its face value; this debt can be discounted to as low as 5 to 30 cents on the dollar.

Debt conversions are often described as win-win situations because the creditor gets some immediate cash payment for an otherwise unrecoverable debt, the debtor saves scarce foreign exchange, and the investor (NGO) obtains more local resources than in a regular foreign-exchange transaction.

One feature that is increasingly becoming a characteristic of debt-for-nature swaps is the establishment of a fund in the forested country's domestic currency—in the case of Uganda, the Uganda shilling would be used to finance the preservation of the forest.

This debt-for-nature option raises several important concerns, namely

1. Will Uganda renege on the agreement and, several years down the line, go ahead and plant sugar due to lack of enforceability of the agreement?

2. Will Uganda use its reduced indebtedness to qualify for more loans and implement other environmentally unfriendly programs, so that the net debt reduction of the debt-for-nature swaps is small, if not zero?

It is clear that a better grasp of the value and proper pricing of the Mabira forest and its use as an underlying asset in any financial contract is just one important example when exploring development options in a modern world. Other options exist, particularly in the field of biotechnology and genetics. But I will confine myself to offering the example of debt swaps as one of various ways that preserving the Mabira forest could lead to economic development and industrialization. Debt swaps make more funds available for development programs with the proviso that corruption is controlled. In this regard, it is only prudent to look into debt swaps in more detail, and the Paris Club Debt Swap Clause in particular.

The Paris Club Debt Swap Clause

The Paris Club debt swaps, or debt conversion, clause was introduced in 1990 for lower-middle income countries whereby part of the consolidated debt may be reduced through debt swaps. This clause was extended in 1991 to Severely Indebted Low-Income Countries (SILICs) to benefit from concessional terms. The Heavily Indebted Poor Countries (HIPCs) Initiative appeared in the mid-1990s replacing SILCs.

Debt swaps are voluntary options open to both debtors and creditors provided for in the Paris Club Agreement Minute. The conditions for Paris Club debt swaps, agreed upon in 1991 and modified in 1996, are as follows:

-   ODA: no limit on the amount that can be swapped
-   Officially insured commercial debt: swaps within the limit of 20 percent of the total debt (officially insured commercial debt) or up to SDR 15 to 30 million, whichever is higher, with the maximum amount (SDR 15 or 30) determined on a country-by-country basis.

In most cases, Paris Club swaps for HIPCs involve officially insured commercial debt, because most of the creditor countries seem to systematically cancel ODA debt for HIPCs with practically very few exceptions.

Within the Paris Club framework is the possibility of conditional swaps. These are bilateral transactions negotiated between a debtor country, such as Uganda, and a creditor. These transactions involve the cancellation by an official creditor of a liability in foreign currency in exchange for a local currency counterpart fund to be invested in specific projects mutually agreed by the debtor and the creditor.

Linking the conservation of Mabira to debt conversion could open up avenues for development not yet fully explored. In quantitative terms, debt conversions can become a source of additional environmentally friendly development funds for civil-society organizations, but it is important to stress that the sums involved here are small. However, with a strong microcredit/loan program targeting the very poor, a little can go a long way, as long as a coordinated development plan and strategy is in place.

Anyway, the bulk of conversions (40 percent) have been debt-equity swaps implemented by banks and international companies. Debt-for-development swaps have generated approximately US$300–US$450 million in local currency, which, compared with the total annual ODA flows of approximately US$60 billion (in 1994) has amounted to a modest addition to development funding. The biggest investors are UNICEF and World Wildlife Fund (WWF).

These are not new concepts, and they can be applied to saving Mabira. The programmatic links between the Save the Mabira lobby and international bodies such as WWF have got to be developed and strengthened.

Environmentalists are not the enemy; Museveni should understand that. Through debt swaps, environmentalists and governments have worked together to strengthen the capacities of civil-society institutions. For example, in the Philippines, the Foundation for the Philippine Environment is an environmental trust fund established in 1991 by a partnership among Philippine NGOs and community-based organizations, the Philippine government, WWF-US, and the United States Agency for International Development (USAID).

The Foundation is structured as an endowment fund that receives its resources from several debt-for-nature transactions. The initial endowment was the equivalent of US$10 million, and overall funding comes from a US$25 million commitment from USAID to fund debt-for-nature swaps.

The foundation is registered as a private, nonstock, and nonprofit corporation and is governed by an eleven-person board of trustees with a broad representation from three major geographic regions (Luzon, Visayas, and Mindanao). Its endowment is currently invested in Philippines Central Bank, earning interest at market rates. Only the interest income accruing from this investment may be used to fund projects and programs. Most debt-for-nature swaps conducted by WWF and Conservation International, among others, have been in Latin America. We now live in an information age, and closer ties between Ugandan environmentalists and civil society with experience of implementing debt-for-nature swaps can and should easily be developed.

In regard to Latin America, Costa Rica presents an interesting case. The country established an environmental trust fund (the National Parks Foundation) to finance the purchase and management of its forests and other protected areas. While the national park service (equivalent of Uganda's Wildlife Service), which works closely with the Forestry Department within the Ministry of Natural Resources, Energy, and Mines, receives very little by way of budgetary allocation from the state, it is relatively well funded, mostly from foreign benefactors through the National Parks Foundation.

Since 1987, the foundation has been able to generate funds of over the equivalent of US$40 million through debt-for-nature swaps. This was two-thirds the value of all funds raised worldwide by mid-1991 in the so-called third world.

The reason I mention Costa Rica and debt-for-nature swaps is not so much that this is an effective way of reducing all Uganda's external debt (Costa Rica was only able to cancel about 2 percent of its external debt through debt-for-nature swaps), but because it is certainly a sustainable way of preserving our forests and environment.

Debt-for-nature swaps were able to raise badly needed funds for environmental conservation, but despite its positive attributes, this mechanism does not offer all the answers and could arguably contribute to inflationary pressures if done on a large scale, as the result could be increased government deficits in local currency. This is not foreseen in the case of Mabira; the funds involved would be minuscule compared to Uganda's debt and national budget.

A criticism about this mechanism is that government is, in effect, turning over much of its financial, administrative, and political responsibility for protecting the environment to foreign-based institutions—although in theory, most swaps are run through a consortium of government staffers and local civil-society groups. But in Uganda, this handing over of responsibility is seen as a positive, as government is now viewed as corrupt and unresponsive to the vast majority of Ugandans.

Civil-society groups are demanding better governance not only of the environment, but also of the entire socioeconomic and political spectrum, through pressure groups such as the Buganda Tuli mu Kulya, NGO Forum, Advocates Coalition for Development and Environment, and the Save Mabira Crusade, just to mention a few. It is the failure of government that is opening up civil-society dialogue about innovative forest protection initiatives.

A number of civil-society organizations now exist that are uniquely placed to implement debt-for-nature swaps, carbon offsetting, and environmental protection in partnership with such government institutions as the National Environmental Management Authority (NEMA), National Forestry Authority (NFA), and the Uganda Wildlife Authority (UWA), and local government structures, namely the District Environment Committee, the Local Environment Committee, the District Environment Office, and District Technical Planning Committee. These civil-society organizations include, for example, the Kabaka Foundation and Buganda Cultural and Development Foundation (BUCADEF), among others.

Debt-for-nature swaps are not the only way of utilizing the forest without destroying it. A number of innovative new exotic instruments have been developed, such as the Capital Protected Forestry Carbon Credit Note and the Discount Certificate on CO_2, which value forests as carbon sinks. The interesting thing is that many of these instruments do not contradict the government's decentralization policy that recognizes that environmental resources are best managed at the district and community level.

The World Bank has also been active in the carbon market. Its main mechanism for promoting reduced emissions from deforestation and forest degradation (REDD) is a scheme launched in 2007 called the Forest Carbon Partnership Facility (FCPF). Under this scheme, the World Bank works with tropical countries to assist them to achieve readiness for REDD. A World Bank senior natural resources management specialist stated when the scheme was launched that "The facility's ultimate goal is to jump-start a forest carbon market that tips the economic balance in favor of conserving forests."

However, after the 2008 global financial and economic crisis, innovative and potentially high-risk financial mechanisms may not be the path to follow, particularly in a country with weak regulatory capacity. A growing tide of speculators and many scholars are critical of the whole entire carbon trading market; Patrick Bond, Director of the Centre for Civil Society, University of KwaZulu-Natal, is on record saying, "I think in fact that many of these emissions markets are full of chancers." Nevertheless, it is important that we discuss them and the carbon market in general as an option in a knowledge-driven economy.

After all, the carbon market remains the dominant official response to climate change worldwide. This market has attracted large global investment banks such as Goldman Sachs, Credit Suisse, Merrill Lynch, BNP Paribas, Citigroup, and Barclays, as well as energy traders, private equity funds, and hedge funds. The volume in trade is over US$100 billion. Paul Collier, professor of Economics and Director of the Centre for Study of African Economies at Oxford University, has pointed out that the potential value of the carbon-trading rights could be "a staggering $720 billion per year—an annual Toxic Assets Recovery Program."

The main reason carbon trading is mentioned is so that government can "think out of the box" and realize that other possibilities exist. Of course, environmentalists know that trading forest carbon alone will not address runaway climate change, and several NGOs and networks have campaigned to expose the inefficiencies of trading the carbon stored in forests. (These include Friends of the Earth, World Rainforest Movement, Greenpeace, Global Witness, and the Rainforest Foundation, just to mention a few.) Nevertheless, Uganda is behind the curve when it comes to carbon trading.

In June 2010, Kenya announced plans to establish a regional carbon emissions trading scheme to steer Africa's carbon market. The finance minister, Uhuru Kenyatta, in his budget speech to Parliament on June 10, made it clear that Kenya intended to be the continent's carbon-credit trade hub. He said that a carbon-credit investment framework would help streamline conservation efforts and alleviate poverty, and this also could potentially attract billions of Kenyan shillings annually. Many Ugandan environmentalists believe that Uganda should be leading the carbon-trading initiatives on the continent, given our geographical position in terms of regional ecosystem networks and sink/outlet or central distribution center for ecosystem dynamics; but alas, while others lead, we follow, and we prefer to use military might to loot and pillage.

In a knowledge- and information-based economy, it is crucial that environmentalists and social activists keep abreast of trends in different fields. It is of paramount importance, for example, to understand the social studies of finance, the growth of the derivative markets since the 1970s, and the new asset class, if only to understand how the world values our resources. The lack of understanding the value or interest, strategic or otherwise, of a given resource is a story of the exploiter and the exploited.

The State of Environment Report for Uganda (2008) is cognizant of the challenge of integrating environmental costs and benefits into key economic indicators. President Museveni's GDP figures have not been greened. A knowledge-based Ugandan economy requires the greening of national accounts to reflect proper and correct reflection of the costs of environmental degradation in national economic indicators, including GDP and GNP.

Greening our national indicators ensures that the contribution of the environment is accounted for and that any negative effects are taken care of in good time. Monocultural agriculture, such as planting sugarcane, could lead to degradation of soil resources and biodiversity loss. Studies estimate that biodiversity loss and degradation of soil resources amount to Ushs 506 billion per year and Ushs 225 billion per year, respectively.[23]

As the saying goes, a little knowledge is a bad thing. The Mabira giveaway is based on a little knowledge of the value of the Mabira forest and the impacts of its destruction. An open discourse among all stakeholders can do wonders for information sharing, resulting in an informed course of action that benefits the citizens of Uganda and the environment.

---

23   Source: Emerton and Muramira

Chapter 8

CONCLUSIONS

This is the moment when we must come together to save this planet. Let us resolve that we will not leave our children a world where the oceans rise and famine spreads and terrible storms devastate our lands ... This is the moment to give our children back their future. This is the moment we stand as one.

Barack Obama,
in a speech in Berlin, Germany,
July 24, 2008

The Mabira giveaway has to be viewed within a wider context of the region; not only does possible harm of the giveaway affect other countries, but the giveaway may also not make business sense in view of wider regional markets. Natural and comparative advantages combined with investment and application of technology among other sugar-producing nations will surely determine the viability of the Mabira giveaway.

Contrary to what the president says, environmentalists are not "enemies of progress"; rather, they are patriotic Ugandans who do not wish catastrophic harm to their country and have no qualms with giving land to businesses if such an approach is utilized efficiently and in an environmentally sustainable manner. But the destroying of parts of the Mabira forest for

79

what in the long run may not be sustainable is unacceptable to most Ugandans.

What is the way forward? Well, dialogue should be encouraged, and different alternatives should be explored, with all being given equal consideration. It is important that both sides hear each other out.

The Mabira forest is far too valuable to destroy by planting sugarcane. It is only when one understands the true value and importance of forests in general and Mabira in particular that one knows that it ought to be protected.

The plan for sugar plantations in the Mabira forest has to be reviewed within the wider context of regional markets (EAC, COMESA) and the competition within them. Natural and comparative advantages combined with technology will surely determine winners and losers in the marketplace. Within the EAC, the three states of Tanzania, Uganda, and Kenya are collaborating in identifying new high-yield varieties so as to be competitive in global markets. However, within the EAC, the potential of Tanzania to dominate the East African market diminishes any potential gains the president believes will accrue from destroying Mabira.

All patriotic Ugandans want policies that will lead to sustainable development. The environmentalists are thinking holistically and within timelines that are generational. Many Ugandans are wary of government and the roughshod manner of implementing policy. Environmentalists advocate a more participative process of formulating development policy: a partnership between government, civil society, and other stakeholders. Strong partnerships are needed to address the issue of environmental degradation; it is because those partnerships do not exist that outrage is expressed in demonstrations. Barack Obama once said, "True partnership and true progress requires constant work and sustained sacrifice. They require sharing the burdens of development and diplomacy, of progress and peace. They require allies who will listen to each other, learn from each other and, most of all trust each other."

The Mabira forest is far too valuable to destroy, and its importance to Uganda and the Great Lakes region is not fully appreciated. Furthermore, studies show that Uganda may not be able to compete with regional states in producing sugar. It is therefore not only reasonable but prudent to adopt precautionary approaches to Uganda's industrialization policy by halting any plans to destroy Uganda's forest and biodiversity.

In neighboring Kenya, the effects of monoculture and the destruction of the Mau forest are now evident. The Mau forest is a catchment area for most of the Kenyan and Tanzanian rivers, including the Makalia and Nderit Rivers, as well as the River Njoro, which is the main source of water flowing into Lake Nakuru.

Lake Nakuru is famous for being the home and breeding site of the lesser flamingos. However, at the time of writing, approximately eight hundred thousand flamingos have deserted the lake. Why? Because the lake is drying up due to diminishing water flows from the lake's catchment area, namely the Mau forest.

One of the causes of forest destruction in Kenya is the collusion of politics and agrocorporatism whereby the interests of politicians and large-scale farming merge to acquire valuable forestland to be exploited for profit at the expense of the environment. In Brazil forests are destroyed to make way for cattle ranches; in Kenya it was for tea estates; and in Uganda it is for sugar.

According to the Mau Task Force report, a number of top officials of former president Moi's government, sitting members of Parliament (MPs), permanent secretaries, and parastatal chiefs were each allocated twenty hectares on the basis of an individual settlement program. In response to the public outrage concerning the misuse of the Mau forest, former president Moi, in a press conference at his Kabarnet Gardens home on December 2, 2009, stated that he saw no fear of an environmental disaster, as tea was as "friendly to the environment" as trees were.

It is this kind of mentality whereby the political leadership assumes national resources belong to no one in particular and are there for them and their cronies to exploit. It is the obligation of today's generation to fight for the interest of succeeding generations by restoring our forests. The interesting difference between Kenya and Uganda in regard to fighting deforestation is that in Kenya, the responsibility for prudent, sustainable environmental management is being led from within government by Prime Minister Raila Odinga; whereas in Uganda, the fight is being championed by political opposition parties and civil-society organizations demanding politics of obligation and good governance.

The efforts to redress the failings of government in regard to the environment in Uganda and the East Africa region as a whole, as seen in the Mau and Mabira, are indicative of bad governance, corporatism, and the greed of the ruling class. The good news is that we the citizens of East Africa, and in particular Uganda, have reached a tipping point whereby a growing awareness of environmental injustices and the transborder impacts of many environmental crises has galvanized the public to fight back.

The response against the government's environmental policy is increasingly being combined with other socioeconomic issues and has led to an increased willingness to mobilize and engage government. This has culminated in the rise of a nascent social movement with strong roots in the oppositional political parties.

It is now apparent that environmental issues cannot be separated from questions of social justice. President Museveni treats environmentalists as marginal, deranged enemies of progress; this thinking is of days long gone. The management of the environment is now a mainstream political and socioeconomic issue that cannot be ignored.

The Mabira demonstrations highlighted a new kind of nationalism that takes the politics of obligation seriously. A new paradigm shift is now evident whereby loose partnerships between institutions and citizens are being forged, creating a more dynamic and varied concept of nationalism that demands transparency, accountability, rule of law, human rights, good governance, and sustainable development.

Environmental justice, social justice, and an accountable government are what the citizens of Uganda are demanding. Unlike in Kenya, where Raila Odinga is fighting his own party and government from within the body politic, Ugandans have had to devise other methods to ensure environmental justice. What Ugandans have done is link wider political campaigns to the sustainable use of our national and human resources.

In conclusion, I quote from Dian Fossey's journal. The last entry reads, "When you realize the value of all life, you dwell less on what is past and concentrate on the preservation of the future." This is good advice for all Ugandans.

Bibliography

Bazaara, Nyangabyaki. "Decentralization, Politics and Environment in Uganda." Environmental Governance in Africa Working Papers, No. 7. Washington DC: World Resources Institute, 2003.

Collier, Paul. *The Plundered Planet.* Great Britain: Allen Lane, 2010.

Daily Monitor Newspaper of Uganda (www.monitor.co.ug)

Dunn, John. *Setting The People Free: The Story of Democracy.* London: Atlantic Books, 2005.

Emerton, L., and T. E. Muramira. "Uganda Biodiversity: Economic Assessment." Prepared as part of the Uganda National Biodiversity Strategy and Action Plan by the World Conservation Union (IUCN) and the National Environment Management Authority (NEMA), 1999.

"Final Report of United Nations Panel of Experts on Illegal Exploitation of Natural Resources in DRC," 2002.

Food and Agriculture Organization of the United Nations (FAO). "Law and Sustainable Development since Rio: Legal Trends in Agriculture and Nature Resources Management," 2002.

Food and Agriculture Organization of the United Nations (www.fao. org).

Ghani, Ashraf, and Clare Lockhart. *Fixing Failed States: A Framework for Rebuilding a Fractured World*. New York: Oxford University Press, 2008.

Gore, Al. *Earth in the Balance: Ecology and the Human Spirit*. New York: Rodale, 2006.

Gore, Al. *The Assault on Reason*. New York: Penguin Press, 2007.

Greenpeace (www.greenpeace.org) Greenpeace is an independent non-governmental global campaigning organization that acts to change attitudes and behavior, to protect and conserve the environment and promote peace among other things by campaigning for sustainable agriculture by protecting biodiversity and encouraging socially responsible farming.

Hawken, Paul. *The Ecology of Commerce*. New York: CollinsBusiness, 1993.

Kazoora, Coornelius, James Acworth, Charles Tondo, and Bob Kazungu. "Forest-Based Associations as Drivers for Sustainable Development in Uganda." *IIED Small and Medium Forest Enterprise Series* 15. Edinburgh, UK: International Institute for Environment and Development, 2006.

Kiss, Alexander, and Dinah Shelton. *International Environmental Law*, 2nd ed. New York: Transnational Publishers, 1994.

Makinda, Samuel M. "Human Rights, Humanitarianism and Transformation in the Global Community." *Global Governance*, 2001.

Moyini, Y., and T. E. Muramira, "The Cost of Environmental Degradation and Loss to Uganda's Economy." Prepared for IUCN, The World Conservation Union. Kampala: Uganda Country Office, 2001.

Mwagiru, Makumi, and Okello Oculli, eds. *Rethinking Global Security: An African Perspective?* Nairobi: Heinrich Boll Foundation, 2006.

Mwakatobe, A., and C. Mlingwa. "The Status of Tanzanian Honey Trade—Domestic and International Markets." Tanzania Wildlife Research Institute (www.tanzanigateway.org), 2005.

Mwenda, Andrew. "Foreign Aid and the Weakening of Democratic Accountability in Uganda." Cato Institute, 2006.

National Environment Management Authority (NEMA). State of Environment Report for Uganda, 2008.

National Environmental Management Authority (NEMA). "Localizing Global Environmental Conventions: Opportunities for Integrating Four Selected Conventions in Planning Processes in Uganda," 2002.

New Vision Newspaper of Uganda (www.newvision.co.ug)

Ochola, Samuel Agonda. *Leadership and Economic Crisis in Africa.* Nairobi: Kenya Literature Bureau, 2007.

Pearce, Fred. *The Last Generation.* London: Transworld Publishers, 2006.

Power Tools (www.policy-powertools.org), a website introducing power how-to ideas that marginalized people and their allies can use to have a greater positive influence on natural resources policy.

Soto, Carlos Rodriguez. *Tall Grass: Stories of Suffering and Peace in Northern Uganda.* Kampala: Foundation Publishers, 2009.

The *Beaver County Times* (www.timesonline.com), a daily newspaper published in Beaver, Pennsylvania, United States.

The *Daily Nation* Newspaper of Kenya (www.nation.co.ke).

The *East African* Newspaper (www.theeastafrican.co.ke)

The *Observer* Newspaper of Uganda (www.observer.ug).

Toffler, Alvin, and Heidi Toffler. *Revolutionary Wealth.* New York: Currency Doubleday, 2006.

Toulmin, Camilla. *Climate Change in Africa.* London: Zed Books, 2009.

Transparency International (www.transparency.org), a global civil-society organization leading the fight against corruption. Transparency International brings people together in a powerful worldwide coalition to end the devastating impact of corruption on men, women, and children around the world.

Tudela, Fernando et al., eds. *La Modernizacion Forzada del Tropico: El Caso de Tabasco—Proyecto Integrado del Golfo?* Mexico: El Colegio de Mexico, 1990.

Uganda Community Tourism Association (www.ucota.or.ug). UCOTA exists to help poor communities improve their lives through the sale of handicrafts and the provision of accommodation, guiding, and cultural performances. Every time you buy a UCOTA craft or service, you are helping a UCOTA member to help themselves.

United Nations Development Programme. *Human Development Report 1994.* New York: Oxford University Press.

Worthington, E. B. *Uganda Protectorate, A Development Plan for Uganda.* Entebbe, Uganda: Government Printer, 1949.

Yew, Lee Kuan. *From Third World to First: The Singapore Story: 1965–2000.* New York: HarperCollins, 2000.

Index

China, 9

Churchill, Winston, 38

CITES (Convention on International Trade in Endangered Species of Wild Fauna and Flora), 4, 29

Citigroup, 77

civil disobedience, ecological, 36

civil liability, 14

civil-society groups, 73, 75–76, 82

climate change, 2, 4, 14, 16, 17, 23, 31, 40, 56, 77

Climate Change Convention, 31. *See also* UN Convention on Climate Change

"climate refugees," 23

climate variations, history of, 20

climate-related disasters, 18

Coca-Cola, 8, 47–49

coffee, 7, 22

Collier, Paul, 77, 85

collusion, of politics and agrocorporatism, 81

COMESA (Common Market of Eastern and Southern Africa), 62, 64, 80

"common concern of mankind" concept, 29

common responsibility, 56

community tourism, 49–50

Conference on the Human Environment (Stockholm 1972), 28

"confused groups," 50

Congo. *See* DRC (Democratic Republic of Congo)

consensus, need for, 38

Conservation International, 74

Convention on Access to Information, Public Participation in Decision-Making and Access to

Justice in Environmental Matters (Denmark 1998), 37

Convention on Biological Diversity (CBD) (1992), 2, 4, 25, 29, 39–40. *See also* Biodiversity Convention

Convention on International Trade in Endangered Species of Wild Fauna and Flora (CITES), 4, 29

Convention to Combat Desertification (CCD), 40

corporatism, 82

corruption, 28, 36, 54, 75

Corruption Perception Index (CPI), 54

Costa Rica, 74–75

cotton, 7

Council of Europe, 57

CPI (Corruption Perception Index), 54

Credit Suisse, 77

crisis management, 18

cronyism, 35

cylcosporin, 26

D

Daily Monitor, 8, 9, 18, 54, 85

Dakar, 7

David-Logoro, Kitara, 16

debt conversion, 72–73

debt swaps, 72–73

debt-for-development swaps, 73

debt-for-nature swaps, 71–72, 74–75, 76

Declaration of Principles for the Preservation and Enhancement of the Human Environment, 28

Declaration on Environment and Development, 2

deforestation
in Brazil, 31

campaigns against, 34
climatic change impacts due to,
 68
in DRC, 66
fighting of, in Kenya, 82
fighting of, in Uganda, 82
in nineteenth-century industrial
 development, 70
and REDD, 76
degenerative development, defined,
 3
democracy, 37, 38, 44
democracy movements, and
 environmental movement, 35
Democratic Republic of Congo
 (DRC), 3, 15, 27, 30, 31, 36, 65,
 66
demonstrations
 reason for, 80
 of Save Mabira Crusade, 21, 34,
  36, 39, 44, 59, 82
Department of Disaster
 Preparedness, 17
Department of Meteorology, 40
derivatives, 69, 78
desertification, 40, 41, 53, 56
Development Plan for Uganda
 (1949), 22–23
differentiated responsibility, 56
digitalin, 26
dimethylsulfide, 30
disaster relief, 18
Discount Certificate on CO2, 76
District Environment Committee,
 76
District Environment Office, 76
District Technical Planning
 Committee, 76
DRC (Democratic Republic of
 Congo), 3, 15, 27, 30, 31, 36, 65,
 66

drought, 20, 23, 31, 32, 41, 51, 53
"dynamic equilibrium," 24–25

E
EAC, 80
Earth in the Balance (Gore), 25, 86
East Africa, 9, 16, 29, 51, 53, 62,
 65, 82
Eastern Equatoria State (Sudan), 3
Eastern Europe, 35
ecological civil disobedience, 36
ecology, Ugandan understanding of,
 25
economic liberalism, 47
ecosystems
 benefits of research on, 26
 and chaos theory, 24
 core ecosystems, 12, 32
 diversity of, 32
 and human rights, 34
 of Mabira forest, 51
 and precautionary approach, 50,
  57
 preservation of, 7
 sustainable use of, 29
 Ugandan understanding of, 25
 value of, 66
ecotage, 36
ecotourism, 26, 43, 49
education, in Uganda, 5–6
EIA (Environmental Impact
 Assessment), 53
Einstein, Albert, 25
El Niñas, 16
El Niños, 16, 17, 18, 21–22
electricity
 lack of, 12
 production of, 10, 31
elite capture, 36, 63
emergency preparedness, lack of, 17
employment

demand for, 82, 83

environmentalists as advocates of, 22

and participatory consultation, 38

principle of, 51, 53–54, 57

and stewardship of the environment, 35

Gore, Al, 25, 35, 69, 86

Great Lakes region, 29, 31, 53, 59, 81

greed, 11, 35, 40, 66, 82

green issues, 49

greening, of national accounts, 78

Greenpeace, 77, 86

Gross Domestic Product (GDP), 12, 47, 54, 63, 78

H

harm. *See also* risks and hazards

and principle of precaution, 57

responsibility to avoid causing, 51

threat of, 14–15, 17, 51, 57–58, 79

Hawken, Paul, 39, 86

Heathrow Airport, 6–7

HFCS (High-Fructose Corn Syrup), 48–49, 64

high-yield varieties, 80

HIPC (Heavily Indebted Poor Countries), 72

holistic interconnectedness, 32, 80

honey and beeswax, production of, 69

Horn of Africa, 53

household organic waste, 31

human development

and the environment, 40

Ugandan understanding of, 25

Human Development Report (UNDP), 43

human rights, 23, 34, 39, 44, 48, 51, 54, 58, 59, 83

human security, categories of, 43–44

hydroelectric power, 31, 32, 53

hydrological cycle, 30, 32

I

ICJ (International Court of Justice), 3

ICT (information and communications technologies), 62

IDP (Internally Displaced Persons), 23, 55

IDRC (International Development Research Centre), 16

IMF (International Monetary Fund), 46

imports

cooking oil and tallow, 9

savings from, 6, 10

India, 9, 48, 62

indigenous people, rights of, 2

industrialization

at expense of the environment, 47

and infrastructure, 64

nineteenth-century compared to twenty-first-century, 15, 31, 42, 49, 62

Uganda's quest for, 55

industries. *See also* factories

versus agriculture, 7

development of, 23

in Namanve, 8

as sine qua non of protecting the environment, 11

information and communications technologies (ICT), 62

information and justice, access to, 4, 37, 38, 50, 54, 58

Innovation Fund (UK), 64

institutional fragmentation, 40

Movement), 3, 5, 17, 19, 21, 22, 34, 36, 39, 43, 44, 63, 64, 65, 70
Nyerere, Julius Kambarage, 46

O

Obama, Barack, 79, 80
obligation, politics of, 82
ODA (Overseas Development Assistance), 72, 73
Odinga, Raila, 82, 83
OECD (Organization for Economic Cooperation and Development), 46
Ogoni, 33
Onyango-Obbo, Charles, v
Operation Iron First, 3
organic waste (household), 31
Organization for Economic Cooperation and Development (OECD), 46
Organization of American States, 57
Otim-Nape, G. W., 16
Our Common Future (World Commission on Environment and Development), 52
outrage
   as expressed in demonstrations, 80
   over Mabira giveaway, 34, 54
   over misuse of Mau forest, 81
Overseas Development Assistance (ODA), 72, 73
Owens Falls Dam (Nalubaade), 32
Owor, Martin, 18
Oxford University, 77

P

palm trees, 9
paradigm shift, 22, 29, 82
Paris Club Agreement Minute, 72
Paris Club debt swap (debt

conversion) clause, 72–73
participatory consultation, 38, 54, 80
PEAP 2004/5-2007/8 (Poverty Eradication Action Plan), 62
personal profit, 66
Philippines, 74
Philippines Central Bank, 74
plantation farming, 63
political power, 39
political violence, and environmental violence, 33
politicization of the environment, 33
politics of obligation, 82
postdamage control, 14
post-disaster relief, 16
poverty
   eradication of, 52, 53
   global target for reducing, 46, 47
   riots as cry against, 36
Poverty Eradication Action Plan (PEAP 2004/5-2007/8), 62
precautionary principle and approach
   adoption of, 81
   application of, 4, 15, 51–52, 56–57
   compared to wait-and-see approach, 17
   environmentalists as advocates of, 16
   European Communication on Precautionary Principle (EU, 2000), 14
   implementation of, 38
   importance of, 20
   as integral to sustainable development, 14
   and Museveni's presidency and legacy, 23

in New Delhi Declaration, 50
as possible answer to address
worst-case scenarios, 13
reason for adoption of, 51
support for, 39
precipitation. *See* rain(s)
predamage control, 14
president (Yoweri Museveni). *See*
Museveni, Yoweri (president)
preventive measures, 19, 20
principle of precaution, 57. *See
also* precautionary principle and
approach
Principles of International
Law Related to Sustainable
Development, 50–51
probability, 15
progressive Uganda companies, 47
"proper" pricing, 68
public participation, 57–58

Q

quick-profit route, 15
quinine, 26, 28

R

Rainforest Foundation, 77
rain(s)
and continental interiors, 41
destructive, 17
and forests, 30
Ramsar Convention, 40
reactive environmental strategies, 67
reconstruction, 16
REDD (Reduced Emissions from
Deforestation and Degradation),
76
reforestation, 70
rehabilitation, 16
renewable energy sources, 31
Report of the World Commission

on Environment and Development
(1987), 44
research, Uganda compared to other
countries, 63
responsibility, common and
differentiated, 56
Revolutionary Wealth (A. and H.
Toffler), 61, 88
rights of future generations, 1
Rio de Janeiro Conference on
Environment and Development
(UNCED) (1992), 2, 13
Rio Declaration on Environment
and Development (1992), 29, 45,
51, 56, 57, 59
rioting, over Mabira giveaway,
33, 35–36, 39. *See also*
demonstrations, of Save Mabira
Crusade
risks and hazards. *See also* harm
management of, and sustainable
development, 44
of "possible harm," 58
and precautionary principle, 14,
15
River Nile, 31
River Njoro, 81
Robert Schuman University of
Strasbourg, 57
Robespierre, Maximilien, 37
Roosevelt, Theodore, 24
rubber, 28
rule of law, demand for, 83
Russia, 63
Rwampara, 11
Rwanda, 30, 33, 62
Rwenzori Mountains, 16

S

Saro Wiwa, Ken, 33
SARS (Severe Acute Respiratory